Lennon and McCartney

HR

Lennon and McCartney

Malcolm Doney

Omnibus Press
London/New York/Sydney/Cologne

Exclusive distributors:

Book Sales Limited
78 Newman Street, London W1P 3LA, England
Book Sales Pty. Limited
27 Clarendon Street, Artarmon, Sydney, NSW 2064, Australia

© Malcolm Doney 1981, 1982

First published in UK by Midas Books in 1981
This edition published in 1982 by
Omnibus Press
(A division of Book Sales Limited)
78 Newman Street, London W1P 3LA, England

ISBN 0.7119.0005.1
UK Order No. OP 41540

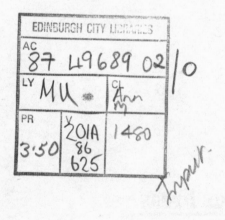

Set and printed in Great Britain
by Billing and Sons Limited
Guildford, London, Oxford, Worcester.

Acknowledgments

My thanks to Jacqui Cooper, who typed from my scribble (Dave, you can have your wife back now); to Tim Dowley for making it all possible; to *Crusade* for latitude; and to Steve Turner for research suggestions. Even more thanks and love to my wife Meryl, for patience and encouragement.

Contents

Introduction

I was just short of thirteen years old when I first heard the Beatles. It was 'Please, Please Me', released in January 1963. I remember seeing them on the 'Thank Your Lucky Stars' programme, bobbing and grinning on a TV screen in the back room of the newsagents on the corner of our street. I was in the shop to buy sweets, but I came out with an undying image of the Beatles.

It never occurred to me then that I would ever write about any of them, and even now it seems slightly impertinent, because the difference their music has made soars above any perceptions I might have to offer. But, as I point out in the book, Lennon and McCartney, or their songs at least, have become public property. For those who, like myself, grew up with the sound of their songs, Beatles' music has become part of me. Memories awaken the music, and music awakens the memories.

But this is not a nostalgia book. It is an attempt to see Lennon and McCartney as part of their time, as people who shared the experiences and lostness of a generation who were trying to come to terms with the world they found themselves in. I trace their individual stories from birth until the present time, or in John Lennon's case up until his cruel death on December 8, 1980.

I have tried to sort truth from legend, and trust that I have placed a proper value on their songs and the complex of influences that brought them to life.

My best wishes go to the McCartney family, to Yoko Ono and Sean. I hope I have done you justice.

Malcolm Doney, *London, June 1981*

1 Working-Class Heroes

Liverpool was down but not out . . . The majestically shabby city had been hit hard by World War II. One of Hitler's major targets because of its port and naval dockyards, it had a gap-toothed look, with bomb sites scattered across the face of the city.

But the port was still alive. In the 1950s freighters and tramp steamers chugged in and out of the Mersey and, significantly, trans-Atlantic liners still plied between Liverpool and New York. Their significance lay not in the ebb and flow of passenger traffic but in the souvenirs brought home by the liners' Liverpudlian deckhands.

These seasoned travellers with their 'men of the world' air formed a link with North America that was to prove of dynamic importance to the life of Liverpool's youth. It was a link that would help stir up a phenomenon never seen before or since. They brought home records—not any old records but wild, noisy records by black rhythm and blues artists, the like of which had hardly been heard before. The discovery of such uncompromising, exciting music was a vital key to the surge of R&B music that appeared in Liverpool in the late 1950s. Eventually, it was to affect John Lennon and Paul McCartney—and hence The Beatles.

John Winston Lennon was born (so legend has it) in the middle of an air raid on October 9, 1940. James Paul McCartney was born on June 18, two years later. They were not to meet until July 1957, when Paul was taken by a school friend to see a group called The Quarry Men perform at a garden fête at St Peters parish church in Woolton, a suburb of Liverpool.

1

They and the other two Beatles-to-be were Liverpudlians, part of a post-war generation growing up in what was, in many respects, a new world. Their recollections and experiences of the war were minimal. What they found, as children and as adolescents, was a world of peace—a prosperous consumer society intent on progress and the gathering of material wealth.

Liverpool in the 1950s was not all that different from any other major British city. It had its slums, its commercial district, its low-life, its bohemia, its suburbs and its subsidised housing. In the post-war years, blitzed as it was, Liverpool still had a thriving commercial and industrial life. The process of slum clearance, which wrenched the heart out of the city and stacked it upright in high-rise columns, was on its way, but was not yet wholesale.

In common with the rest of Britain, those who had fought in the war made efforts to take hold of the coming prosperity to line their nests after more than a decade's hardship. Their children, however, failed to see things in the same light. Parents felt they had seen enough trouble with the depression and the war. What they wanted now was a comfortable life, a few luxuries and peace. It was understandable.

But their kids turned their backs on it. It wasn't the idea of being consumers that they didn't like; teenagers were the arch consumers of the period. It was the idea of peace and quiet that failed to inspire them.

The 1950s saw the development of a peculiar animal—the teenager. Of course, there had been teenagers before, but no one had actually noticed them as a separate group. There were either girls or women, boys or men. The long, tortuous period of adolescence was not recognised as particularly distinctive. In the 1950s, rock'n'roll ensured that it was.

There was, in post-war Britain, a hang-over culture from the pre-war 1930s—the days of dance bands and crooners. During the war, fashions, like everything else, had been frozen. Now, in the heady days of peace and optimism, that music spoke of a bygone era. As the new youth grew up, as rationing gave way to a burgeoning consumer boom, young people shook off the past their parents tried to hand down to them. They wanted excitement, freedom—a good time. Shuffling about on the dance floor or darts and shove-halfpenny did not fit into their aspirations.

2

But rock'n'roll did. When the first raucous sound of Bill Haley and The Comets filtered across the Atlantic, it meshed well with the feelings of the young. Here was something wild and physical enough for them to launch themselves into. Then came the teddy boys in their long Edwardian-style drape coats with narrow lapels and velvet collars, drain-pipe trousers ending just short of the ankle from whence peered day-glo socks of disastrous hue shod in 'brothel creepers'. Bootlace ties adorned necks which in turn supported the ted's crowning glory: the D.A. This hairstyle was an aggressive cockscomb plumage, held stiff and glistening by liberal applications of grease. The hair was swept up at the side and down at the back to meet in a duck-tail effect — the Duck's Arse markings which provided its short-hand title. This quivering cantilever or quiff, sculpted into a gravity-defying over-hang, was the final dandyism.

It was these Fifties creatures, who sprang out of the closet in cities all over the country, who first took rock'n'roll to their hearts. Their looks and behaviour were a slap in the face to their parents' generation — an inarticulate rebellion against the more prudent values that had come through the war years.

It was against this background of growing teenage independence and rebellion that John Lennon and Paul McCartney grew up. The teds with their consummate style set the image pattern they aspired to and rock'n'roll was the music that caught their adolescent imaginations, becoming an obsession and setting them on that much sought after but rarely found route to the loot.

John Lennon's father, Fred, who his mother Julia had married in an apparently light-headed moment in December 1938, was a ship's waiter. He was away when the war broke out and made only brief appearances at home in 1940 and 1942 and then disappeared. John Winston Lennon was brought up by Julia, with the help of four sisters, until he was eighteen months old. Then, with Fred having apparently deserted ship, the shipping company stopped paying Julia his wages and John became a problem. Julia found another man and Mimi Stanley, one of her sisters, was only too keen to take the baby under her wing.

Julia was a happy-go-lucky, light-hearted soul, not sold on the idea of responsibility and family life. But Mimi, married to

George Smith, who owned a small farm and dairy in Woolton, had a developed sense of order and respectability. No less fun-loving than her sister, she nevertheless wanted a more stable framework to her life. She and kind, quiet George took John into their semi-detached, 1930s home, 'Mendips', in Menlove Avenue, Woolton. Julia would visit her son most afternoons and, though in later years she came to be a constant source of fun and laughter, it was Mimi who provided the constancy and affection — his upbringing. Mimi remained the one stable element in his life for years. She loved him, scolded him and mothered him.

Lennon's relationship with Mimi was, it seems, a fiery one. Always a restless spirit, John was never easy to control — a strong-willed boy, and inevitably a leader among his peers. But he was often content to go off for the day with Uncle George, sometimes leaving a note behind for Mimi.

At the age of four, John went to Dovedale primary school near the now famous Penny Lane. A reasonable if unremarkable pupil, he loved writing, drawing and singing. Lennon particularly remembered throwing himself into Richmel Crompton's *Just William* books about a ne'er-do-well scamp of an eleven-year-old who was perpetually in trouble. *Alice in Wonderland* and *The Wind in the Willows* were devoured with equal enthusiasm. He wrote 'Jabberwocky' type poems and acted out the characters of this favourite book. He also sang in the choir at St Peter's church, Woolton.

Around the age of seven he began writing books of his own, including new 'William' stories with himself as hero. In particular, he wrote a series called *Sport and Speed Illustrated*, 'edited and illustrated by J. W. Lennon', which contained stories, cartoons, jokes and drawings.

No one seemed to take much notice of his creative output, a fact that seems to have irked him (though Mimi kept many of his books). He said later: 'People like me are aware of their so-called genius at ten, eight, nine . . . I always wondered, why has no one discovered me? In school, didn't they see I'm cleverer than anybody else in this school?'

Lennon's big mates at Junior school were Pete Shotton, Ivan Vaughn and Nigel Whilley. Together they became a regular little gang. Lennon, the undisputed leader, and the others told of their scrapes and escapades: they threw clods of earth at trains going into the tunnel at Garston; they shop-lifted sweets; they rode on the bumpers of trams and had a great time of it.

Lennon was brought up strictly and was allowed two major treats a year. One was a Christmas visit to the Liverpool Empire for the pantomime; the second was a Disney film in the summer. Another place that figured was Strawberry Fields — a Salvation Army Children's Home where, each summer, there was a garden fête.

Lennon remembered them vividly, though possibly with the kind of corrective thought hindsight gives: 'We (he and Nigel and Pete) would go there and hang out or sell lemonade bottles for a penny. We always had fun at Strawberry Fields. So that's where I got the name. But I used it as an image. Strawberry Fields for ever.

' "Living is easy — with eyes closed. Misunderstanding all you see" . . . Let's say in one way I was always hip. I was hip in kindergarten. I was different from the others. I was different all my life. The second verse goes, "No one I think is in my tree". Well, I was too shy and self-doubting. Nobody seems to be as hip as me, seems to be what I was saying. Therefore, I must be crazy or a genius, "I mean I must be high or low", the next line. There was something wrong with me, I thought, because I seemed to see things other people didn't see. I thought I was crazy or an egomaniac for daring to see things other people didn't see. As a child, I would say, "but this is going on!", and everybody would look at me as if I was crazy. I always was so psychic or intuitive or poetic or whatever you want to call it, I was always seeing things in a hallucinatory way.'

Visionary and poetic his inner vision may have been, but his public persona was more physical. He fought his way through Dovedale primary, asserting his ascendence by coming out on top. When, at the age of twelve, John Lennon changed to Quarry Bank Grammar School, the foursome was divided. Both Nigel and Ivan went to separate schools but Pete Shotton and John remained together. Their friendship became more firmly bonded.

Quarry Bank, though not an old institution, was a grammar school of the traditional type. Masters wore gowns and there was a strong house system and a reverence for academic distinction. John arrived in 1952 and never quite fitted in.

Both bright, Lennon and Shotton nevertheless gravitated to the bottom of the 'C' stream. It appears that almost from the start John was determined not to bend himself to the rules of the institution. He rejected the standards demanded of him and

5

became the figure familiar to so many schools of the type — the intelligent, irrational rebel who refuses to be brought round. Peter Shotton was not a leader but remained a willing ally to John's schemes, skipping school, playing practical jokes, avoiding work. They found themselves constantly in detention, often caned and perpetually in the masters' bad books.

Predictably, Art and English were the only subjects where Lennon made any impression and, even there, his interest was not of orthodox academic expectations. He continued to pen acerbic little poems, doodles and cartoons. Not until his teens did music really become important to him.

Just before John reached the age of thirteen, his Uncle George died suddenly of a haemorrhage. Around the same time, his mother came back into his life. Although she had always kept an eye on John, after the first eighteen months it had been from a distance. Julia lived only a short way from his Woolton home with a waiter of a rather nervous disposition (Pete and John dubbed him 'Twitchy'), and they had children of their own. Julia kept open house for the two Quarry Bank miscreants and John found in his mother a liveliness and devil-may-care attitude to life that matched his own. As they grew up, the boys spent more and more time at her house.

But John differed from his mother in that his non-conformism was marked by a brooding aggression and a streak of nastiness with which he asserted his authority. Friends of the time think that his spirit of independence was positively encouraged by Julia, herself the black sheep of the family. Together they laughed at school, conventions, and, most important, at John's own rebelliousness. But Lennon knew his own worth. His fight with authority had taken him, by the time he was fifteen, to 4C. He accepted the demotion with resignation but had no time for the 'thickies' of the lowest stream.

It was obvious that he needed some diversion. Eventually, it came — in the unlikely form of Bill Haley and The Comets. Lennon had had no taste for formal music lessons, though he had learned the harmonica. There was no musical motivation: Lennon, like many of his contemporaries, listened with half an ear to Johnny Ray and Frankie Lane, but the slick show business vacuity of it all made no real impression. This was music tailored for the previous generation.

Then suddenly, out of nowhere, Bill Haley and The Comets exploded. This rough, ham-fisted amalgam of white country music and black rhythm and blues grabbed British youth just as it had American. The music was wild, exciting, unorthodox. It had a driving beat which pushed people to their feet. Teenagers responded — not instantly, but with a growing recognition that this was *their* kind of music. When parents and other authoritarian figures professed themselves shocked and disgusted at this noise, it set the seal on rock'n'roll as the private possession of youth.

As the teddy boy cult grew in Liverpool, fifteen-year-old Lennon saw in their drapes and drainies a sense of style which he could aspire to. Until around 1956, John Lennon was still an onlooker to the world of teds and rock'n'roll. Then, 'Heartbreak Hotel' was released and Elvis Presley stole his heart away. From then on, as far as John was concerned, there was no going back. Bill Haley had provided a certain stomping clumsiness; he had no image — the tartan jacket, the round friendly face and the kiss-curl were altogether too cute for rock'n'roll. Elvis was the supreme God-like figure both boys and girls could look up to. He was all flash. His sultry good looks and arrogant appearance turned girls to jelly while his patina of tough delinquence made him a hero-figure for the boys. And, of course, there was his deep, brooding voice with its breathy emotion and raw energy backed by the promise of fiery music. He was the King.

The real pied piper was rock'n'roll, said Lennon. 'When I heard it I dropped everything else. It was instinctive. Rock'n'roll music gets right through to you without having to go through your brain. Rock'n'roll music goes right to the gut!'

John cajoled Mimi into buying him a second-hand guitar. He learned to play banjo chords taught him by Julia and, perhaps for the first time in his life, he applied himself to the task. Sore fingers notwithstanding, he would lean for hours on the front porch trying to wrench a tune out of a 'guaranteed not to crack' Spanish guitar.

By now, Mimi was seeing even less of him as he spent more and more time at Julia's. Mimi forbade him to dress in teddy boy style, but Julia was happy to taper his baggy school trousers and buy him his first coloured shirts. To escape Mimi's wrath he would leave his home in conventional gear and change into full dress at Julia's.

This desire to imitate was endemic to the youth of the period. But rock'n'roll, simple and basic as much of it was, was not something that was easily picked up by would-be musicians. What started many a rock'n'roller of the period off was the arrival of a phenomenon that *was* imitable: skiffle. In 1956, Lonnie Donnegan, the banjo player from Chris Barber's revivalist jazz band, had a hit with 'Rock Island Line'. Originally an earthy blues number, when Donnegan sang it, it became something of a joke. But the accompaniment of washboard and simple bass brought hope into the hearts of thousands of teenagers who leapt for guitars, washboards and thimble, constructed tea-chest basses and hurried into action.

John Lennon was not much different. He may have had greater aspirations, but for the moment skiffle was a start. Although without much musical talent or inclination, Pete Shotton was included in his group, playing washboard. Curiously for such an anti-school pair, they named themselves The Quarry Men. Nigel Whalley and Ivan Vaughn alternated on tea-chest bass.

John was the only one remotely like a musician and still he knew only banjo chords. But his repertoire was growing. Auntie BBC refused to play rock'n'roll for some while but the delicious, if blurred sounds of Elvis could be heard, late at night, via the commercial station Radio Luxembourg. Alongside Elvis, Lennon discovered the raw delights of Chuck Berry and Little Richard — a rich vein of musical gold.

The Quarry Men found other recruits: Rod Davis on banjo, Eric Griffiths on guitar and an older boy, Colin Hanton, who had that most prized and awe-inspiring possession, a full drum kit! But Lennon was from the beginning the undisputed leader, a scowling, Elvis-style front man.

Already he had begun to write songs — not so much as a conscious creative exercise but because none of them could afford to buy records (so as to copy down the words). The only way to learn new songs was from the radio. Most of the lyrics were indecipherable so John would make up his own to fill in the gaps. No one noticed.

Gigs were few and far between — mostly skiffle contests and youth club hops. Their performance was scrappy; and so too was the atmosphere. Fights would break out — and it wasn't always the audience that started them!

Then, one day in the summer of 1957, St Peter's parish church, Woolton held its annual fête. A skiffle group was needed to attract the younger element. Who else should they choose but local boys, The Quarry Men? Ivan Vaughn, then a pupil at the Liverpool Institute, decided he would bring a mate of his along to meet John. He could play guitar quite well. His name: Paul McCartney.

Jim McCartney was a cotton salesman who'd risen from the ranks of the lowly clerks to a respectable if still humble position. His wife Mary was a health visitor. Jim had been the leader of the Jim Mac Jazz Band, a semi-pro outfit which played locally during the 1930s. During the war he transferred from the cotton exchange to Napiers engineering works. He married Mary in 1941 and in 1942 their first son, James Paul, was born in Walton General Hospital.

Their first home was furnished rooms in Anfield. From there, they moved to a small council house in Wallasey, and then on to Speke, a new council estate. Jim now had a job as inspector for the Liverpool Corporation's refuse collection department. The pay was poor and Mary returned to work as a health visitor.

After their second son, Michael, was born she went into full-time domiciliary midwifery on the new estate — the house went with the job. She was keen and conscientious and was called out most nights.

Paul did not have the ingrained aggression and rebelliousness of Lennon. He was accommodating, pleasant and impressionable but determined and independent. A natural student, he did well at Stockton Wood Road primary school. When the school became overcrowded, he and Michael moved to Joseph Williams primary school at Gateacre.

McCartney steered away from trouble by diplomacy and tact. Revenge was taken but on the quiet. He tells a revealing story of his habit of sneaking into his parents' bedroom and ripping the lace curtains, just a little, at the bottom, in response to punishment.

Paul went to the Liverpool Institute High School for Boys, adjacent to the Art College and close to the unfinished Anglican Cathedral. The academic standards demanded of him were no strain, but he claims to have had little interest in what he was doing — a particular disappointment to his father who hoped for academic distinction for his eldest son.

Jim returned to being a salesman in the cotton industry but, already, the mills were being hit and the money was still poor. When Paul was thirteen, the family moved to Allerton, a mere two miles from John Lennon's home. It was another council house and another domiciliary post for Mary McCartney, though she later returned to health visiting.

When Paul was fourteen, tragedy struck the family. Mary McCartney began to suffer from pains in the breast. She struggled on in silence for some while, but eventually saw a specialist. Cancer was diagnosed and she died shortly after. The boys, affected but not so devastated as their father, were moved to an aunt's house while Jim tried to prepared himself for a new, difficult life as a single parent. Jim McCartney became both mother and father to the two boys, providing for them on his own meagre wage.

Paul had been given an old trumpet by an uncle and he tried in vain to make sense of the instrument. He never managed and eventually lost heart. He had been interested in what passed for pop music since the age of twelve and, at the age of fourteen, apparently out of the blue, he asked his father for a guitar. At first, Paul could not master the instrument. Then he discovered that, being left-handed, he had to reverse the strings and hold the guitar the other way round. Just like Lennon, once he'd got the instrument, he was lost. Nothing else seemed to matter. He would practise, practise, practise, until his fingers were numb.

Michael McCartney has suggested that Paul's musical determination might well have stemmed from his mother's death, and the new phase of his life certainly seems to date from that time. But whether it was escape or compensation, it was to set the pace of his life for years to come.

He listened to skiffle and learned the hits. He, too, was impressed by the first inroads that rock'n'roll made, and was sent into ecstasy by the king, Elvis. The Everly Brothers made an impact on him, too — an enthusiasm he shared with school mate Ian James. They would stroll around together in white jackets (after the song, 'white sports coat') and black drainpipes. Paul did not join a group but made attempts to get Michael and Ian together for sessions. A year later, in 1957, Paul and Michael made their first appearance together at a talent contest at Butlin's holiday camp at Filey, Yorkshire. They sang 'Bye-bye love' and Paul finished with 'Long Tall Sally'. They didn't win.

One of his friends at school was Ian Vaughn, Lennon's mate. Vaughn was still in awe of his aggressive Quarry Bank ally and brought only his most impressive contacts to meet him.

Knowing that Paul was already showing qualities of musicianship that marked him out from the others, he was given the dubious honour. Ivan knew The Quarry Men were playing at the summer fête at Woolton parish church. He took Paul along.

At their first meeting Lennon and McCartney treated each other with cautious respect. Paul thought The Quarry Men were quite good, even though John could play only banjo chords. After the performance, when Paul did his student party-piece — a full-blooded Little Richard impression — and showed them the chords to a number of songs The Quarry Men only vaguely knew, it was John's turn to be impressed. Not least of Paul's virtues, in their minds, was the fact that he could actually tune a guitar — an art The Quarry Men had never mastered.

John was uncharacteristically slow in making a decision. Paul was good, but was he a threat? But he *was* good. Yes, they'd ask him to join. It was Pete Shotton who bore the request and Paul agreed. The Quarry Men's next gig was at the conservative club in Broadway. After the performance Paul, who had recently begun to write, sang two of his own numbers to John.

It was Paul's song-writing that started John off. Although he had already used his creativity in adapting other people's material, he had never really assembled his own. Paul gave him the incentive and, from then on, the two spent hours in each other's company, trying new material as they doggedly pursued their song-writing. At first the songs were banal and unoriginal, but they improved slowly. They met at Paul's house when his Dad was at work, or at Julia's — often in school time. Hunched over their guitars they would teach each other new chords — a lengthy process, since McCartney was writing left-handed and everything worked backwards to John. The two became the focus of The Quarry Men; John was still the leader but Paul was a dominant influence. The others were make-weights.

Peter Shotton left soon after when a drunken Lennon smashed the wash-board over his head. It was less out of malice than a convenient way out for both of them. Pete Shotton was no musician and he knew it.

In their mid-teens, John Lennon and Paul McCartney did not stand out as particularly unusual. Admittedly, Lennon was aggressively anti-social and anti-authority; he had a nice line in sharp, even savage jokes, and he was imaginative. McCartney

11

was bright in a more orthodox sense and with a demon determination and application to his chosen enthusiasm — the guitar. But that could have been said of any number of intelligent post-war kids who failed to see the point of the world that had been constructed for them out of a war.

What they were quick to see was the opportunity within it. They did not feel any burden of responsibility to society — any need, at this stage, to make a contribution. What they saw in rock'n'roll was the opportunity of freedom, a good time, and a chance to be admired. However, it seems they harboured no illusions about the possibilities of making their living from music, although they undoubtedly dreamed of it. Neither did they look further than their own immediate interests.

But John had to do something. By 1957, his school career was coming to an end — a finale without qualifications. He failed all his exams, but, at the suggestion of Quarry Bank's newly appointed headmaster, and on the evidence of his unorthodox talent, he applied to and was accepted at Liverpool Art College. Now he could wear his teddy boy colours during the day, unhampered by school uniform, although such dress was officially disapproved of by the college.

Paul was still at school — literally round the corner — taking his 'O'-levels and entering the sixth form, but with progressively less interest. The Quarry Men were disintegrating, however, due to pressures of school work and the prospect of employment. Waiting in the wings was an acquaintance of Paul's — a shy, silent, gawky fourteen-year-old with a passion for guitars. His name: George Harrison. No one, other than Paul, took him seriously, and he would follow the group around to their hops and dance-halls. Now and then he would be given the chance to play with slow, painful concentration. Eventually, he became a fixture.

Then tragedy struck once more. John was somehow stuck in the lettering department of the art school, a class requiring a precision and doggedness Lennon didn't have. The Quarry Men and Paul were taking up a lot of time and the relationship with his mother was growing as he spent more and more time with Julia, 'Twitchy' and the children.

John was at Julia's house when a policeman came to the door with the news that his mother was dead. On her way home from Mimi's she'd been knocked down by a car and killed instantly.

John was devastated, but he had long trained himself not to show 'unmanly' emotions and he allowed himself no public grief. However, his demeanour became more cruel, his temper more erratic and his drinking serious. Girls seemed to get the worst of the treatment, while he and Paul were drawn closer. Julia's death left deeper, invisible scars that he was not able to come to terms with until much later.

Meanwhile, Lennon met two important people. Stu Sutcliffe was a very talented student painter who shared John's love of image and style and communicated an excitement for modern poetry, painting and the world of ideas. Cynthia was a quiet, shy suburban girl whose middle-class manner at first made her a figure of fun to Lennon and his mates in lettering. But a relationship developed that became stronger than any boy-girl attachment he had ever had. Cynthia was soft, yielding and understanding, unlike the more brittle Liverpool womenfolk he had been out with.

Stu Sutcliffe won a prize in the prestigious John Moore's Exhibition held annually in Liverpool's Walker Art Gallery. With two thousand entering, most of them artists of some experience, Sutcliffe's £65 prize was no mean achievement. It would have been characteristic of Sutcliffe to have spent it all on paints. But John had impressed him as much as *he* had impressed John. Stu went out, bought an electric bass and signed up with The Quarry Men.

The music scene in Liverpool was changing. By now, the Cunard Yanks, in the wake of Elvis and Little Richard, were bringing in the music that had been the initial inspiration for rock'n'roll in the States — rhythm and blues. These sounds, even more tough, raw and exciting than commercial rock, found a ready audience among the Liverpool skiffle groups. Second-hand, the music came down to Lennon and McCartney. R&B sounds could be heard on the juke boxes in the teddy boy haunts around the 'Pool's dockland. Local R&B groups were already starting up.

By now, all The Quarry Men had electric guitars and they had to rely on hasty and probably dangerous wiring jobs by George to put them through the microphone system. For a time, Ken Browne, a short-lived member of the group, supplied a ten-watt amplifier at a time when The Quarry Men were playing a new teenage club, the Casbah, owned by a Mrs Best. Later,

Stu Sutcliffe persuaded the Art College students' union to purchase an amplifier for the boys to use on the premises for rehearsals and college dances.

Before Stu Sutcliffe joined the group (who were without a drummer after their regular had gone to join another group) they were given their first major public opportunity. 'The Carroll Levis Discovery' TV show held auditions in Liverpool for a programme to be broadcast live from Manchester. The Quarry Men got through the audition and later set off for Manchester with a new name: Johnny and The Moondogs. You had to have a leader they thought, and who else but John? The Moondogs, they decided, had more class than The Quarry Men, which had uncomfortable connotations they wanted to leave behind. But they didn't do well, and in fact had to leave the show before reappearing at the end for the vital register of applause in which placings were made, in order to catch the last bus home. It was a severe blow to their confidence.

Still more engagements were coming their way. Local bands were beginning to call themselves beat groups now and it was from this stem that the awful pun The Beatles came about. For a long while, they made no public acknowledgment of their choice of title, perhaps because most people reacted with derision. They only changed it to The Silver Beatles when the chance of a big audition came up.

Through Alan Williams, owner of the Jacaranda coffee bar where the band used to hang out, they were given an audition at the Blue Angel Club, which Alan Williams also owned, for promotor Larry Parnes. Parnes was an almost mystical figure, having made famous a bevy of British versions of American rockers. He loved to give them descriptive names: Tommy Steele, Billy Fury, Marty Wilde and Johnny Gentle. Parnes was looking for a backing band for Billy Fury's Northern and Scottish dates. The cream of Liverpool's beat groups were there: Rory Storme and The Hurricanes, Cass and The Casanovas and Derry and The Seniors. Each had their own fan following, but the newly dubbed Silver Beatles had nothing, not even a resident drummer. Tommy Moore was essentially temporary and he was late for the session.

The drummer from The Casanovas sat in for them but Parnes was not greatly impressed. Since he was looking for cut-price musicians, they were eventually booked for a two-week tour in Scotland backing Johnny Gentle. Great excitement — a real job!

The tour was not the road to stardom as they had hoped. The fortnight was remarkable only for the fact that Tommy Moore got concussion and his teeth loosened when the gear in the van fell on him after the unstable Johnny Gentle had rammed a parked car. However, when they returned to Liverpool (Lennon and Sutcliffe having skipped college and McCartney his 'A'-level revision) their stock was a little higher locally. Moore left — leaving his kit — and The Silver Beatles were now on the regular circuit of ballrooms and town halls and usually managed to get a stand-in from the audience to play drums. Alan Williams was managing them in an informal way.

With work slow, they returned to playing the Casbah club. The resident group there was The Black Jacks, whose drummer, Pete Best, was the son of the Casbah's host and proprietor, Mona. The Bests lived in the house in whose basement the Casbah was settled. Pete was a good-looking boy and a firm local favourite. He had turned down the chance of teacher training college, deciding instead to be a professional drummer.

In the summer of 1960, Alan Williams, who was now working part-time for Larry Parnes, as well as running clubs and coffee bars, acting as manager to one or two groups and promoting local concerts, met Bruno Koschmider. Koschmider owned the Kaiserkeller in Hamburg's notorious red-light district — the Reeperbahn. He was interested in taking loud English rock'n'roll groups for his seedy clientele and, after much to-ing and fro-ing, he accepted The Beatles (they had dropped the superfluous 'Silver') on a two-month contract for £15 a week each. They were to play at Koschmider's second club, the Indra.

John had left home now and was installed in a crumbling bedsit with Stu Sutcliffe in Gambler Terrace, a stone's throw from the college. His student career in tatters because of laziness, drink and lack of interest, there was nothing to stop him. Paul had to talk his dad round, and, after a pep talk and a united, if diplomatic, attack by Paul, brother Mike and Alan Williams, Jim McCartney was persuaded. Stu Sutcliffe was persuaded to leave college for a year, rather than start immediately on a one-year post-graduate teaching course. George promptly left his less-than-inspiring job as a window dresser for Blackler's department store. But they still needed a drummer.

Pete Best was jobless. His dreams of a showbiz career had evaporated when The Black Jacks split up. There he was, with a brand new drum kit and no work when Paul McCartney phoned up and asked would he like to go to Hamburg. Yes, he would.

In the end, ten people crammed into Alan Williams's cream and green minibus: The Beatles; Williams and his Chinese wife; Williams's West Indian business associate, who rejoiced in the nickname of Lord Woodbine; a German waiter from Soho (who was returning to Hamburg to become Bruno Koschnider's interpreter), and Williams's brother-in-law.

With no work permits, posing as students, The Beatles eventually arrived in Hamburg. Wide-eyed, they surveyed the streets and the city centre, reconstructed since the war.

Lulled into a false sense of security by the Kaiserkeller, a big prosperous club, the Indra came as a depressing shock to The Beatles: it was a tatty cellar with absolutely no charm. Their living quarters were worse: one room with a window and two boxes without. All three were filthy and there was no water. They were housed behind the screen of Koschmider's movie house, the Bambi. They were expected to use the cinema's toilets for ablutions, and sleep through the booming sounds of gunfire or orgasm, depending on what film was showing behind the thin walls. If The Beatles wanted romantic squalor — they'd got it.

From here they emerged to play four and a half hours each night and six on Saturday and Sunday. At this stage, not many of John and Paul's songs had made their way into The Beatles' regular repertoire. But there was, even then, a gutsy freshness and enthusiasm about what they were doing. They had discovered black music, the roots of the rhythm and blues sound that had been at the base of rock'n'roll. This they combined with songs by Carl Perkins, Elvis and even some sickly ballad standards.

Awed and, at the same time depressed, by their surroundings, initially they were self-conscious, unsure of themselves and entirely lacking in conviction. Still, it wasn't easy, playing to a dozen boozy seamen who plainly ignored them. But traditional Scouse cockiness showed through in the end. Koschmider, disappointed in his latest scruffy, gauche English signings bawled at them, 'Mak show! Mak show!' John Lennon caught on, and began to leap about, Gene Vincent-style. Immediately, audience interest quickened.

From then on they made show, four, six and sometimes eight hours a night. With a repertoire built for a one-hour show, they began to draw the numbers out — sometimes to twenty minutes in length! They found that the German audience liked noise and a big beat, so they turned up their amplifiers and persuaded Pete Best, still the outsider in the group, to pound his drums mercilessly. Meanwhile, the rest beat their feet like demented elephants to provide a stomping, gut-shaking rhythm whose repute soon attracted a large following.

They had to play hard to gain any kind of attention. Their audiences were not the impressionable teenagers of Liverpool's dance halls. These were seamen, dockers, servicemen and whores. Fights were not uncommon, but these were not teddy boy rumbles; they were full-blooded saloon brawls of western-style proportions. Through it all, The Beatles kept playing, John and Paul out front throwing their bruised, cracked voices over the sounds of smashing glass and furniture. They were getting good, too — welded into a unit out of the need to survive. Their playing and primitive stage-craft were improving.

Hamburg ushered these still innocent youths into a tumbling underworld far beyond their previous imaginings. Sex was easy if squalid — there were plenty of offers. Off-stage, they were shown the decadent offerings of the low-life: lady wrestlers squirming in mud, the strippers, the blue movies, the transvestite bars and the bewildering array of prostitutes who disported themselves in every shape, size, design and apparel — the consumer durables for off-duty hedonists.

The Beatles did not throw themselves into the mêlée but remained detached, taking what they needed as it presented itself. There was a surfeit of all but money, food and sleep. As dawn broke, they would walk zombie-like to their den and sleep for maybe two or three hours before the first film of the day would bring them to a kind of wakefulness.

Often, they would spend the afternoon at the British Sailors Society, a mission where they were treated as any other exile Britons. They could eat basic, English-style food and there was a piano where John and Paul continued to work out songs, each offering a chord here, a phrase there. It was a kind of oasis from the desert madness of the nights. By now they had discovered the traditional night-life crutch — pep-pills. They were recommended Preludin, a brand of German slimming pill with a high amphetamine content. Prellies, as they were known, both reduced appetite and, when taken in large quantities, produced a bug-eyed hyperactivity. Only Best resisted.

This lethal combination of prellies and alcohol was the diet on which The Beatles existed during those long Hamburg nights. As far as they were concerned, the artificial energy was a positive boon when frenzied leaping and general 'making show' were demanded.

Without prellies Lennon could be loony enough. Stories of his exploits abound — standing in the street in his underpants reading the newspaper, together with other madness and cruelties. John was still the strong, uncompromising, sarcastic leader with the ability to talk himself in and out of trouble in quick sequence. John and Stu were still close, but it was music that was all important and Stu never quite made it; the Lennon-McCartney axis was what made the group work. George, still only seventeen, was often ignored while Pete Best retained an aloofness and independence which was eventually to lose him his place. The others became used to his daytime disappearances. Consequently, he remained on the edge of the unit.

Eventually, Bruno Koschmider showed grudging regard for their success at the Indra and moved them down the Grosse Freiheit (the street where the club stood) to the larger Kaiserkeller. Here, the audiences were bigger, the noise louder and the fights larger. The Beatles, without missing a note, would watch Koschmider's athletic waiters and bouncers converge on and beat up any would-be trouble makers. They believed in fighting like with like.

The band alternated with another Liverpool outfit, Rory Storme and The Hurricanes. The two had 'mak show' competitions, trading lunacy with lunacy and ending up by stomping right through the Kaiserkeller stage. Rory Storme's band included a docile-looking drummer with big eyes and a beard. His name was Ringo Starr.

The Kaiserkeller *was* a step up, but not a large one. They were still playing to the staple, largely male, Reeperbahn crowd who were out for a drink or several, a bit of aggro and some girls. There were still few real rock fans in sight. Normal kids never went near the place and there was a police ban on under eighteens — a fact which seventeen-year-old George always contrived to get round.

But then along came Astrid Kirchherr and Klaus Voormann. Both were young avant-garde ex-art students. Voormann was an illustrator and Kirchherr a photographer. They came from a generation of young, intelligent, middle-class people who became known as *exis* after the French existentialists.

Voormann, after a row with his girlfriend Astrid, went on a stroll that took him off his normal stamping ground into the Grosse Freiheit. A rock'n'roll fanatic with aspirations as a record sleeve designer, he was drawn by the sound of the heavy beat coming from the Kaiserkeller. He was knocked out by the storming music played by a now red-hot Liverpool five-piece. He told Astrid but she refused to go near the seedy part of the city. Voormann returned with a mock-up of an album sleeve design, met the lads and talked to Stu — the artistic one. They became friends.

Astrid was eventually persuaded to come down and she, too, was impressed, especially by Stu. The Beatles were struck by her, with her all-black clothes and severe, cropped hair. They agreed to be photographed. The stark, high contrast prints from the subsequent photographic sessions remain as a graphic record of the developing skill of the image-conscious but still naïve-looking beat group.

Her eventual love-affair with Stuart Sutcliffe is a side issue but what she did was to help, by example, to groom The Beatles into a more cohesive sense of self-image. On a later Hamburg stint, she persuaded Stu to do away with the piled-up grease of the D.A. It was replaced with the low-fringe, combed-forward look of the German high fashion art students. The Beatle hair cut that later flooded the Western world had been created. John, Paul and George soon followed Stu's example.

Most important, Astrid and Klaus shared their enthusiasm for The Beatles with their large circle of friends and brought them to the Kaiserkeller. The grapevine began to work, and soon the burly seamen were supplemented and eventually all but supplanted by a committed bunch of teenagers and early twenty-year-olds who came to the club for one thing — the music.

The Beatles' two-month stint had been extended until, by November 1960, they'd been in the Reeperbahn for over four months. They were still living in squalor on prellies and alcohol. But they had a following. A new, better club, the Top Ten, started up and they were offered a residency. But it was not to be. They were due to open at the Top Ten when the Hamburg police decided one day to examine George Harrison's passport. Finding he was only seventeen and too young to be in a club after midnight, he was told that he could no longer stay in the country.

Shattered, this solemn youth was seen to the train by Klaus and Astrid, whence he departed to his home town. The others filled in and carried on, but not for long. They had left Koschmider's club under a cloud because of contract problems. Pete and Paul returned to the Bambi to collect their gear. A stray match caught some drapes and the small fire caused a little damage. But the police pounced: they were jailed for a few hours and then told they were to be deported. The next day they were on a flight back to Britain.

John and Stu had no alternative but to leave. Stu, who had become a fixture at Astrid's home, had his flight paid for by the Kirchherrs. John was left to struggle home with guitar and amplifier to arrive in Liverpool in ignominy in the middle of the night. The only welcome he received from Mimi was a stream of abuse about his cowboy boots.

Too ashamed to show their faces, even to each other, The Beatles lay low. Having set off for Hamburg and the big time, they had come back exhausted, penniless and unhealthy. The Beatles' future looked about as rosy as Liverpool's famous blackened sandstone buildings on a grey day.

Lennon and McCartney were not even a true partnership. They had come from their separate backgrounds, drifted together, been thrown into intimacy in the wild Hamburg night life, but had come out of it with apparently very little. But what was to spark later was there, dormant, as they kept out of the searching gaze of their fellow Liverpudlians. The shared enthusiasm for rock'n'roll, the joint discovery of this exciting R&B music, the singleness of purpose that saw no alternative to a life in music, the feeling that there was nothing else that mattered — all this was still drawing them together. One disappointment was not going to break it down.

2 Hard Days and Nights

It is easy to lose sight of Lennon and McCartney in the ensuing story of The Beatles, because it was The Beatles as a unit that became popular. It is important to remember, nevertheless, that The Beatles as an entity owed their basic drive and impetus to these two. It is unlikely that The Beatles phenomenon would ever have happened had it not been for the meeting of these two great personalities. They were very different characters and, in different circumstances, could easily have been antagonists. When the two went their separate ways in 1970, the acrimony that developed showed just how different their attitudes were.

It is interesting that John, the only one of The Beatles not brought up in a council house — the only one with what could be called a suburban upbringing — was the one, from the very start, who had a passionate hatred of authority. He was the quickest to react against any kind of control imposed from outside. He was the first to deflate any pretentiousness. He carried an enormous chip on his shoulder and yet felt vulnerable enough to protect himself with a constant show of aggression, cultivating a brutal line in sarcastic put-downs that was to leave many a girlfriend in tears and reduce many an acquaintance to jelly. He was a born misfit.

Paul, on the other hand, though not a joiner, had considerable social skills. He threw himself into whatever he chose to do, and with considerable charm easily became popular. But always, he remained detached. Behind his friendly exterior lurked an iron determination. But his tactics were different. Whereas John would get his way by direct, crushing means, Paul was, as we have seen, more devious. The strategy was somehow classically English — the iron fist in the velvet glove.

Paul was more interested in status than John. He wanted to be recognised as *someone*. But he was, like John, unwilling to seek status through the recognised channels of education and career. Those values were meaningless to both of them.

Their answer to the demands of school and authority was to opt out, right back in the mid-1950s. This was where the two, even before they knew each other, began to join forces. The moment came when they picked up the guitar. Through music, each found a vehicle — not, at this stage, to challenge authority — but to carry their energies and their undoubted creativity.

Rock'n'roll had not yet developed into a music which could attack consciously the values of adult society. The lyrics of The Beatles songs — as much of pop music before and since — were concerned with the frustrations of love rather than the shortcomings of society. But it was rebellious nevertheless. By its very loud, raucous nature, it denied access to the generation brought up before the war. It belonged identifiably to the young. That was why John Lennon and Paul McCartney picked up on it, and the shared obsession for the music was the catalyst that brought the two together.

It took some guts to struggle through those teenage years at the end of the 1950s and into the new decade. They had no money, and took many knocks and a few disasters. Yet, as can be seen in the wake of their first tour of duty in Hamburg, something drove them on.

Again it was Lennon and McCartney who, while leaning heavily on R&B and rock'n'roll records imported from the USA, continued to battle away at their own songs. In both cases, they brought something fresh and new. They did not simply regurgitate the American rock'n'roll anthems they played; they invested in them their own ideas, rejuvenated them. At a conscious level, when they wrote together, bringing a verse or two here, a middle section there, they were trying to imitate. But by so doing, they brought, unconsciously, all their accumulated experiences of life in Liverpool in the 1950s. The bitterness and aggression of Lennon found expression in these songs. McCartney's ability to shrug off life's difficulties with a grin brought its own brittle quality to the music. The results were simple and often banal, but they refused to become carbon copies of the American product. They had a quality of brashness and charm that was pure Liverpool.

Just for a while, those qualities were in short supply. The

Beatles' gloom lasted some weeks. Even when they got back together again, using the Casbah as their base, Paul was not at all sure of the value of returning to the life of a full-time musician. He even tried his hand at a regular job or two — delivering parcels, coiling steel. It lasted only two months.

But the gigs they did perform during this period opened the eyes of the Liverpool audience. The Beatles had left the city in the summer of 1960, a shambling bunch of talented amateurs. They came back as seasoned professionals with a virulent, hard-hitting stage act that split the ear drums and generated a real excitement. Suddenly, The Beatles were a force to be reckoned with.

What John, Paul and the rest had not realised was that, while they were away in Hamburg, the rock scene in Britain had gone to sleep. Elvis was in the army, Eddie Cochran was dead. The wilder sounds of rock'n'roll had given way to the manufactured froth of Fabian, Pat Boone and the rest. British rockers lacked the ability to generate fresh noises, trapped as they were into following whatever came from the States. Too many of the local British bands spent their hours trying to copy The Shadows. But the desire among the teenage punters was still for excitement and hard city sounds.

That was what The Beatles supplied. As local DJ Bob Wooler wrote in the summer of 1961, The Beatles' resurrected original rock'n'roll music, the origins of which are to be found in the American negro spirituals'. Not only did The Beatles resurrect it, they transformed it through their own peculiarly English experience. This was genuinely *British* rock'n'roll.

The Beatles seemed largely unaware of their own potential until December 27, 1960, when they were given top billing at Litherland Town Hall. Gathered to hear the group heralded by the posters as 'The Beatles direct from Hamburg' were fans from all over Liverpool. There was an enormous, enthusiastic audience. John remembered the evening: 'We really came out of our shell and let go. We discovered we were quite famous. This was when we began to think for the first time that we were quite good.' They gave the kind of stomping performance they had been doing in Germany. There was a near riot, and afterwards girl fans chalked messages on their van — the first of many.

Local promoters began to take a more active interest in The

Beatles, and from then on they never really went short of work. It slowly dawned on them that they were better than the rest of the Liverpool groups. Their fans were growing in number, and people began following them around from gig to gig.

In the New Year, they were given a regular lunchtime spot at a jazz club in Liverpool's Mathew Street. Now famous, wrongly, as the birth-place of The Beatles, the Cavern was a dingy, sweaty, wholly squalid little cellar in the warehouse district. It had no acoustics and when packed with young typists, office workers and labourers in the lunch hour, the walls would drip with sweaty condensation.

To The Beatles it became home three or four days a week. In just over a year between January 1961 and 1962, they played 292 times. They established a rapport — albeit extremely informal and sometimes abusive — with their audience that was never to be achieved again. They could eat and smoke while they played, sit down if they felt tired, but all the time they would belt out their hectic but authentic noise.

By early spring 1961, the lure of Hamburg had grown again as groups like Gerry and The Pacemakers returned from a winter season tour with stories of The Beatles' old haunts. Pete Best contacted Pete Eckhorn of the Top Ten club who offered them £40 a week each to return — more than twice what they'd earned before.

Sadder and wiser, they had train tickets and work permits this time, and, of course, George Harrison was one year older. They were welcomed enthusiastically by Astrid, and she and Stu took up where they'd left off.

The nights were as wild as before, if not more so. Lennon's madnesses multiplied — making himself a paper clerical collar and preaching out of a window in a Peter Sellers-style Indian dialect, abusing church goers.

For Stuart Sutcliffe, the romance of rock'n'roll was beginning to fade as he planned a long-term stay in Hamburg. He managed to get a student grant from the Hamburg arts council — largely through the influence of Scots-born sculptor Eduardo Paolozzi, who taught a masterclass in Hamburg and recognised Sutcliffe's talent. For a while, Sutcliffe continued to paint in the day and play with The Beatles at night; but that could never work. Another factor was Paul's growing animosity to the bass player. Paul retained a high musical standard and Stu was still a

24

make-weight as far as he was concerned. He let him know it. When The Beatles returned to Liverpool, Stu stayed on, but he didn't have much longer to run.

He began to complain of headaches and a year later he was dead from a medical condition which meant that his brain was expanding. He died of a haemorrhage. Almost certainly, it was the result of a kick in the head, sustained during a post-gig scuffle.

While in Hamburg, The Beatles cut their first single — as a backing group for British rock singer Tony Sheridan — under the name of The Beat Brothers. They were recorded by a German orchestra leader Bert Kampfaert, whose idea of a 'catchy' number was 'My Bonnie Lies Over The Ocean', played with an oompah and a back-beat. It was a disaster, but it gave The Beatles a certain kudos.

They returned to Liverpool for a warm welcome and a regular routine with the regular Cavern dates. Their music was still rough and ready and Paul and John were still writing songs, but as yet they had not the courage or conviction to make much of these on stage. Instead, they concentrated on importing American songs and adapting them to their own style.

All this time it was John and Paul, the two main contenders, who supplied the initiative, the musical muscle and the dynamism of the group. Admittedly, it was Pete Best's moody good looks that made him the main target of girl fans' attractions. But The Beatles were John's and Paul's baby. George was greatly improved as a musician but he was still, painstakingly, learning the ropes. After Stu left, Paul took over on bass, something he'd wanted to do for some time, something that had been the cause of the friction between him and Sutcliffe.

In July 1961, Liverpool's own music paper was launched. *Mersey Beat* was started by art student Bill Harry and produced by him and his girl friend. From the first edition, The Beatles loomed large in its pages. The arrival of this fortnightly paper was an indication of just how big the Mersey beat scene had become, and a measure of the local fame The Beatles had achieved.

In September, without so much as a word to the others or to the Cavern or other promoters who'd booked The Beatles, John and Paul set off for a week in Paris where they rendezvous'd with Jurgen Vollmer, a German photographer friend of Astrid's and a habitué of German rock clubs. It was an escapade that threatened to break up the group — Peter and George were so disgusted. Once more, it showed the growing bond between the two. They returned, bright and smiling, sporting the 'French' haircut that Astrid had given Stu, but in this instance, it came of the scissors of Jurgen. After some diplomacy by Bob Wooler, now a friend and mentor (he compered their Cavern sessions) and Cavern owner Ray McFall, the unit was brought together. After a while, George had his hair cut the same way. Independent-minded Best did not conform.

It was at the end of 1961 that The Beatles met up with Brian Epstein. Born on September 19, 1934, he was a misfit at a number of day and boarding public schools, and later joined one of the family's furniture stores as a salesman. At this he excelled and his artistic flair proved useful in revolutionising the Epstein's staid window display policy. He caught a taste for acting and was given a place at RADA. But after his fourth term he quit, returning to the bosom of his family. He ran their store in Wirral, but later transferred to the newly acquired electrical and music store in Great Charlotte Street in Liverpool's shopping centre.

He ran the shop with imagination and efficiency and created a city-wide reputation for NEMS (after the North End Road Music Stores — another property owned by the Epsteins). From the very beginning, he threw himself into the business, determined to make the place a success. Before long, a second city-centre store was opened in Whitechapel. They boasted the finest record selection in the North and Brian prided himself on always supplying his customers' needs, however obscure.

This was how, according to the oft-reported story, he came to discover The Beatles. When Raymond Jones, a NEMS regular, entered the store and asked the smart young manager for 'My Bonnie' by The Beatles, he was met with polite interest. Epstein had never heard of them, surprising perhaps, since they were now local folk-heroes. But he made it his duty to find out, especially since two girls asked him for the same record later that day.

At this point, Brian Epstein was living something of a double life. The young executive by day, by night his desires led him elsewhere. Epstein was a homosexual. In Britain, male homosexual acts were illegal, so his exploits were shrouded in some circumspection. He had developed a taste for the 'rough trade' — a factor which was to make his private life precarious in later years. But his night life escapades had never led him into the Cavern.

His enquiries as to The Beatles record drew a blank, but they did lead him to the Cavern. Thinking it good for business, he decided to talk to the group themselves and find out where he could secure some supplies. So in November 1961, at the age of twenty-seven and largely untouched by rock'n'roll — his preference was for Sibelius — Brian Epstein made his way into the grimy depths of the Cavern.

It has been suggested that the sight of the leather-clad Beatles at that lunchtime concert, strutting their arrogant way through a regular set of barn-storming numbers appealed instantly to the night-time Epstein. Here was his fantasy, alive in the daylight. There is no denying that he was immediately attracted to the aggressive meanness of John Lennon, but to suggest that this appeal to Epstein's dark side was responsible for his continued perseverance on The Beatles' behalf is too simple.

It has to be remembered that The Beatles arrived at a time when the ambitious Epstein was frustrated by the limits of the shop and the city. He wanted a wider sphere of operation and a better vehicle for his creative talents. The Beatles were an artistic challenge.

Epstein talked to them briefly that day, but later he invited them to his office to talk management. The Beatles were impressed by his well-to-do appearance and the fact that he drove a Ford Zodiac, very much a status car in those days. At a further meeting, he signed them up for twenty-five per cent of their meagre earnings. He remembered one thing about the foursome especially: they had a 'sort of presence'. It was a quality of group identity, despite the inner tensions and rivalry that they already showed. It was to be a vital factor in The Beatles' success.

There was no doubt about The Beatles' ability to whip up an audience or in the conviction with which they played their music. But they were still, essentially, a small-time club band. Epstein wanted more. So did the group, but they were living from gig to gig without the ability to strategise or take on a wider perspective.

Epstein knew that if they were to get anywhere they needed a

27

more professional attitude. At present, they were eating, smoking and even arguing on stage. They indulged in private jokes between themselves and the first few rows of the audience. He bought them lounge suits from Burtons and produced typewritten memoranda urging punctuality and warning against slovenliness on stage. Lennon in particular was most resistant to these changes, wanting to continue as nature intended; but Epstein found an ally in Paul and eventually John submitted.

Under his guidance, The Beatles' performance became altogether more slick. He persuaded them to work out a balanced programme of songs, something they'd never done before, and got them to cut back on the ad libs. They learned to put on a good show for reporters, remaining polite and playing along with them. Once more, this stuck in John's craw and he later lamented the need to put up such a front. Always the least compromising of the four, he nevertheless realised that such adjustments were necessary if they were to get anywhere.

The pop scene in Britain in the early 1960s was totally dominated by London. Liverpool might as well not exist as far as the record and publishing magnates were concerned. From the start, Brian Epstein found himself swimming against a tide of indifference to his northern group. But, as one of the biggest record retailers in the north, he had some clout with the record industry and tried to use what contacts he had to secure a contract for his boys.

Eventually, Decca expressed an interest and their newest A&R man, Mike Smith, came up to the Cavern. He liked what he heard and invited The Beatles down for an audition. On New Year's Day 1962, they arrived, nervous and overawed, at Decca's recording studios. Playing safe, Epstein suggested that their best bet was to ignore the scores of songs John and Paul had amassed by that time and to concentrate on their slightly eccentric versions of standards. Out of the fifteen songs they played in a state of high tension, severely inhibited by the studio's glowing red recording light and with Paul's voice cracking, only three were written by Lennon and McCartney: 'Hello Little Girl', 'Like Dreamers Do' and 'Love Of The Loved'. For the rest, they played 'Till There Was You', 'September In The Rain', 'Sheikh Of Araby', 'Red Sails In The Sunset' and some rock numbers. To their surprise, Smith seemed pleased with the session and they returned home in high spirits. In the meantime, Smith had second thoughts and signed up a group called Brian Poole and The Tremeloes.

Brian hawked the tapes of the session round to the other record labels but was turned down by Pye, Phillips, Columbia and HMV. No one was interested in a group that sounded unlike any of the current chart material. They felt guitar groups were a thing of the past; solo singers were what they were looking for.

Significantly, Pete Best was the last to know of the failure of the Decca audition. The others knew about it for weeks but never told him. He found out independently. This apparent conspiracy of silence did nothing to help Best's growing feeling that he was not quite part of the club. But those considerations were swept aside as The Beatles prepared for their third trip to Hamburg in April. Epstein, never one to miss an opportunity for a flourish, decided they should fly out to their new booking, the new Star Club in Hamburg. That would look especially good in the pages of *Mersey Beat*.

Just as they were about to leave, their excitement was blasted into gloom and shock at the news of Stu Sutcliffe's death in Hamburg. It shook them all, but they were unable to pause with the pressure of dates to fill and audiences to pacify. Hamburg played host to the usual wildnesses, particularly of John, who seemed about to take leave of his senses, entering into mad competition with other English émigré musicians as to who could be the most extreme. Epstein's typed memos on appearance and presentation were lost in the noisy, drunken atmosphere of the Reeperbahn's night-life.

While The Beatles were making music in Hamburg, Brian Epstein was making a last, desperate bid in London. He had been given the name of the A&R man for EMI's last remaining subsidiary, Parlophone (the other two had turned him down). The man in question was George Martin.

He listened to the acetate Epstein had had made from the Decca tape and was mildly interested. His own label had had most of its success from 'light' music and from the comedy records of Peter Sellers and the like. EMI's big label, Columbia, had Cliff Richard and The Shadows and other top-name pop stars. George Martin badly needed a new act. Could this be it? He decided to give The Beatles a recording test on their return from Hamburg in June.

'Congratulations boys, EMI requests recording session. Please rehearse new material', ran the telegram received from Epstein with much excitement.

Weary from six all-but sleepless weeks in Hamburg, The Beatles arrived at EMI's Abbey Road studios on June 6 for their recording test with George Martin. Once again, their performance was shot through with such awful standards as 'Besame Mucho' and George Martin was only marginally impressed. He gave them an exhaustive run through, hoping to find a new Cliff Richard among them. He did not. But of one thing he was certain, Pete Best was not good enough.

However, he thought the group sufficiently fresh and interesting to sign them up. In fact, he and The Beatles hit it off quite well — a surprise, since the schoolmasterly George Martin was not a natural ally. 'I found them very attractive people; I liked being with them.' However, he did not give Brian Epstein a definite offer until late July, and then it was a mean EMI contract for four titles with the derisory royalty of one pence per double-sided record sold, to be spread across Epstein and the four Beatles. But it *was* a contract.

In the meantime, it seems that (George Martin notwithstanding) Paul and George had already decided that Best ought to go. (John was otherwise preoccupied and was not part of the debate, though he agreed with the move.) The sacking was the result of an accumulation of grievances. Best was a loner and, therefore, not sufficiently part of the unit; the others didn't like that. He had, for instance, always held out against changing his hairstyle into the French-cut Beatle fringe. There may well also have been some sour grapes from Lenno and McCartney, who considered that as front men the focus should be on them. Since Best outshone them in looks, he disturbed the equilibrium. But the fact remains that Best was not a very good drummer. He had been picked up in a hurry on the way to Hamburg first time out. The decision to use him was purely practical and, with the chance of a Parlophone contract, so was the decision to drop him.

They knew immediately who they wanted to replace him: the erstwhile drummer from Rory Storme and The Hurricanes, old adversaries of The Beatles. They knew him well from Hamburg and liked him. They had even played together on an ad hoc session in the recording booth at Hamburg's railway station.

Ringo Starr was born Richard Starkey on July 7, 1940. At the age of six, he had spent a year in hospital following a burst appendix. At thirteen, he contracted pleurisy and was hospitalised again with complications that kept him there for two years. He never went back to school and spent most of the time he should have spent catching up on learning to drum. He changed his name while working with Rory Storme at a Butlin's holiday camp. He was small, bearded and, above his large, sad doggy eyes was a streak of prematurely grey hair.

He was playing at Butlin's in Skegness when John rang him up. Would he join The Beatles? Pay was £25 a week and he'd have to comb his hair forward and shave off his beard, but his side-burns could stay. He says it was the money that made him accept.

John had his own problems. He and Cynthia had been all but living together for some time and that 1962 summer found her pregnant. John, the cynic, the hard man, surprised Cynthia by agreeing to marry her and they were duly wed on August 23. It was not altogether a joyless affair — Lennon played it strictly for laughs, but he had to. Workmen were drilling the road outside and nobody could hear anyone else throughout the ceremony. Afterwards, they found themselves in a restaurant with no licence. Brian proposed the toast — with water!

News of Pete Best's sacking was revealed in the *Mersey Beat* issued on the day of John's wedding. It caused an uproar. The reaction from female fans was more virulent than anyone could have predicted. Petitions were signed, girls staked out Best's home all night. The Beatles were heckled on stage and Ringo went almost in fear for his life.

Around this time Paul had his one and only row with Brian Epstein. A small episode, it reveals something essential about McCartney's character. Brian and the rest of The Beatles came round to pick him up one night, but Paul was in the bath and didn't want to rush out. He shouted for them to wait a few minutes, but they drove on. For once, McCartney refused to be hurried. 'If they can't be arsed waiting for me, I can't be arsed waiting for them. So I sat down and watched telly.' His non-appearance led to a strong argument between him and Brian. But the reason for his petulance was his feeling that he needed to revolt, a feeling that his keenness was being taken for granted. 'I'd always been the keeny, the one who was always eager, chatting up managements and making announcements. Perhaps I was being big-headed at first, or perhaps I was better at doing it than the others. Anyway, it always seemed to be me.' Having made his point, Paul soon reverted to his role as diplomat of the group. 'I realised that I was being more false by not making the effort.'

In September, The Beatles received the call to return to EMI's Abbey Road studios to record their first single with George Martin. Martin had previously been responsible for The Goons' comedy records, as well as the material from the Beyond the Fringe team, whose satire was beginning to attract a cult following in London. Lennon and Martin shared a great love for Peter Sellers and The Goons. John was impressed to find out that George Martin had produced their records. It created an important bond since Lennon was the least likely to take to anyone in a position of authority. And given the power wielded by the EMI producer, Martin was certainly in charge.

George Martin showed good instincts by choosing only three of four songs suggested by Brian Epstein. The standards were rejected, and two of those left were songs which, written out in long-hand by the authors bore the imprimatur 'Another Lennon-McCartney original'. They were 'Love Me Do' and 'P.S. I Love You'. His judgement concurred, inevitably, with that of The Beatles. It was a bold step, since it would not have been too great a problem to raid Tin Pan Alley — the music publishers' ghetto — for a song to fit. But Martin remained true to his instincts, relying on the freshness and simplicity of the Lennon and McCartney compositions.

Ringo was a surprise to George Martin; he'd been told nothing of the change and had already booked a session drummer to stand in for Pete Best. In the end, although both drummers were used, Ringo features on the single's A side — 'Love Me Do'. It had been John's harmonica introduction which had marked it out as a possibility for Martin. They got it right after seventeen takes, and the tapes went off to become The Beatles' first ever single as a group in their own right.

In October 1962 'Love Me Do' was released. Slowly, it crept chartwards, helped by Epstein's brave purchase of 10,000 copies, most of which gathered dust in the storerooms of the NEMS record store. The single hovered tantalisingly around number twenty-seven and then, in December, inched into the

Top Twenty at number seventeen. There had been little or no promotional backing from Parlophone so the fact that it did so well is unusual. The Beatles were ecstatic.

George Martin had selected 'Love Me Do' not because it knocked him out, but because he had thought it better than the rest of the available material. Anxious lest his new-found group should turn out to be one-hit wonders, he set out to find a 'professional' song for their follow-up. EMI's publishing company had nothing. He contacted a small, but imaginative independent, Dick James (later to become publisher of all Lennon and McCartney output). James agreed with Martin that 'Love Me Do' was OK but limited, and played him a song he was convinced was a sure fire hit: 'How Do You Do It'. Martin loved it.

John and Paul did not. They said so boldly when George Martin played them the song in November. The two songwriters, confident in their own abilities, wanted to do another of their own compositions. Martin was at his most schoolmasterly: 'When you can write material as good as this, I'll record it. Right now, we're going to record this.'

The Beatles complied, went into the studio and gave a flat, lifeless performance. Then Lennon and McCartney played George Martin the song they wanted. It was a new version of 'Please, Please Me', a song they had shown him before but not recorded. It had something. Back into the studio they went. First take, The Beatles threw their collective energies into it, and although both John and Paul forgot the words at different times, the virility and enthusiasm of the performance were palpable. 'The whole session was a joy', Martin remembers. He told them through the studio intercom, 'Gentlemen, you have just made your first number one.' 'How Do You Do It' was later to be a hit for Gerry and The Pacemakers, another Epstein protégé group.

The record was not due out until the New Year, and a December trip to the Star Club in Hamburg had been booked for months. With things breaking on the horizon at home, Hamburg's romantic aura had disappeared. Their performance there showed it: their energies were with their thoughts — elsewhere.

1963 began bleakly. The winter in Britain was the worst anyone could remember. But Britain was ready for The Beatles; it was as if the country had been waiting just for them. 'Please, Please Me', the song Lennon and McCartney had fought so hard for, led the way.

There was a mood alive in the 1960s that lacked only a focus to make it sharply recognisable. In the music world, a new generation had grown up. They had been weaned on rock'n'roll, but now, as they entered adolescence, they demanded a new type of rock music that would express *their* experience of living. The old rock'n'rollers were fading and, for a while, there were no heroes to replace them.

Conventional figures of respect and authority were no use to the young. In Britain, the Conservatives were in their ninth year of government with an ageing MacMillan at the helm. 'You've never had it so good,' he told them. It was a voice and sentiment rooted in the past.

The growing undercurrent of satire that surfaced in the Establishment Club, the magazine *Private Eye* and TV show *This Was The Week That Was* all conspired to debunk, to pillory the nation's leaders. Alongside the satirists, there was a strongly critical attitude among bright young intellectuals, many of whom made their way into the world of the media — TV, film, journalism and photography. They began to ask tough questions of establishment figures. They showed the public that these irreproachable chieftains had surrounded themselves with a mystique too often ill-founded.

Nothing did more to support this feeling than the onset of the Profumo scandal, starring, among others, Cabinet minister John Profumo and 'model' Christine Keeler. The Fleet Street bally-hoo that followed let loose a babble of gossip and rumour, avidly devoured by a hungry public.

Watching on the sidelines was the largest group of adolescents the country had ever known. The bulge of the immediate post-war years had now become an army of teenagers. But, in 1960, National Service had been abolished and so, far from being a military army, there was an overbalanced youth population with money to spend and time to spare. The consumer boom had begun.

In these times, how could they believe in the country's leaders? They were figures of fun. The church had lost its muscle and, to a large extent, its relevance. Values were being shot at from every direction. Those who could defend them with enough sense for the discerning and restless youth were few.

So out of the sixties came a rootless, religionless generation. Not so much searching, but lost for direction almost without knowing it. They badly needed some certainty, someone to identify with. They needed someone who could assure them that being young was important and valuable, and that the future was theirs for the taking.

Along came The Beatles, singing Lennon and McCartney's simple songs. Yet somehow they became the embodiment of all those hopes. However you look at it, it's still astonishing that four such unsuspecting characters should be the repository of such hope and belief. But it happened. The question is: did The Beatles happen to British youth or did Beatle fans happen to The Beatles?

As the decade dawned, there were only the faintest indications that anything would happen at all. They had one minor hit and what looked like a good prospect waiting, in the can. At best, they could hope for success, money and fame, however short-lived. Adulation they might get, but who could tell?

On January 12, The Beatles played on *Thank Your Lucky Stars*, ATV's pop programme, in their first ever networked exposure. They sang 'Please, Please Me'. They looked different, fresh and enthusiastic, fringed heads bobbing up and down on stage in an uncoordinated but infectious way. They were no carbon copies of anyone else, they sounded different. This was something new in 'pop', as it became called, and it came from Liverpool. But, *no one* came from *Liverpool*! There was a ripple of interest in a million homes.

The record was released the same month and similar ripples appeared in the music press. Brian Matthew, compere of *Thank Your Lucky Stars* and BBC radio's *Saturday Club*, said they were 'musically and visually the most accomplished group to emerge since The Shadows'.

At the end of January, the *Evening Standard* writer, Maureen Cleave, interviewed them. It was an important piece, giving them a vital toe-hold in the metropolis as their single rose to the Top Ten. She picked up qualities in the foursome that were to be discovered again and again. 'Their wit', she wrote, 'was keen and sharp . . . they look beat-up and depraved in the nicest possible way.' The ripples spread wider. By March, 'Please, Please Me' was number one.

It was time to do an LP. Once again, George Martin's instincts

35

came into play. He refused to follow the usual practice of rushing out an album stuffed with fillers to sell on the basis of the hit single. Instead, he chose a selection of songs from the sets they had played at the Cavern. In an effort to capture the immediacy of their stage performance, he recorded the fourteen-track album in one gruelling thirteen-hour session. Of the fourteen cuts on the album, entitled *Please, Please Me*, eight were Lennon and McCartney songs. What Martin did for The Beatles' music was similar to what Epstein did with their public image. He pruned and arranged, without denying the true character of the sound. The album contained such Lennon and McCartney rockers as 'I Saw Her Standing There', mellow 'MOR', numbers like 'A Taste Of Honey' and, straight out of the Hamburg night, The Isley Brothers' 'Twist And Shout'. A small masterpiece, it was released in late March to warm praise. As yet, there were no fireworks.

But 1963 was The Beatles' year of conquest. Although Beatlemania did not really manifest itself until late in the year, The Beatles had a solid fan following from early on. After 'Please, Please Me' went to number one, so did all their subsequent recordings that year: the EP 'Twist And Shout', then successively, 'From Me To You', 'She Loves You' and 'I Want To Hold Your Hand'. During 1963, The Beatles held the number one spot for no less than nineteen weeks.

The Beatles have been spoken of as a manufactured phenomenon. But this is plainly not true. There was no abnormal publicity for their early records. Right up until around August 1963, the records sold on the quality of the music — the songs of Lennon and McCartney. They managed to catch the imagination of the record-buying pop fans. 'From Me To You', put out before they were names on everyone's lips, sold half a million in advance copies alone. The Beatles toured, first as a double-headliner with Roy Orbison, and then on their own. All venues were packed out, and a black market in Beatles tickets was rife.

Until June, The Beatles still returned to Merseyside in between tours, playing local venues. Their last ever performance at the Cavern was in August. By that time, the music business had finally caught up with the Liverpool scene and record companies signed up practically anyone who could play a guitar. In 1963, there were five number one hits by

Liverpool artists and Liverpool beat music became known universally as 'the Mersey Sound'.

Touring was a relief for the foursome. They were feeling stale in Liverpool, and it was good to break new ground, refreshing to meet new audiences who were already beginning to scream and to mob their heroes. There was too much pressure in the 'Pool, too. They were known too well and widely for them to feel free in what was for them the beginning of a new life. At home, John found himself back in his old ways. In June, at Paul's 21st birthday party, John got into a fight with a local disc jockey, beating him up badly. The DJ sued and John had to settle it with a payment of £200. Secretly, they were glad to turn their backs on Liverpool.

In April John and Cynthia's baby was born. It was a boy. John, in the event, was overjoyed. He named him Julian — the nearest male name to his mother's. But Cynthia and the baby were left to cope alone. John left, first on holiday with Brian and then on tour again.

In August, The Beatles produced their fourth single, 'She Loves You'. 'Yeh, Yeh, Yeh', ended the refrain — a chorus taken up across the nation. Until now, most of their interviews had been with the music or local press. But as the screams grew louder and the mobbing had to be controlled by police, the national press, having exhausted both the Profumo affair and the Great Train Robbery, pricked up their ears.

They found, in The Beatles, natural light-weight copy. In the desire to fill their columns with the wacky goings on of the pop world's newest stars, they helped mould the public image of the group into the four Mersey mop-tops, the cuddly Beatles, the lovable, cheeky urchins from the back streets of Liverpool. The coverage began in the popular dailies, but the quality press followed by the posh Sundays all gave them top billing in their own idiosyncratic ways. By autumn, they were never out of the news.

But it was not just the rumours of cosmic earnings by these callow youths that made them news; nor was it the popularity or quality of their music; it was the weight of their following that got them noticed. By and large, the nationals had failed to recognise the young as a forceful entity in society. They referred to The Beatles and others as 'pop' groups, as if the very term had to be held at arm's length. Slowly, they were forced to realise that these four young men were fostering hysterical hero worship among teenagers — providing an influence and focus for youth such as had never been seen before.

The Beatles gained maximum exposure. In October, they played *Sunday Night At The London Palladium* before an estimated TV audience of fifteen million. Fans now had to queue all night for tickets. But it was on returning from a five-day tour of Sweden later that month that The Beatles themselves realised just how much of an impact they had made: they arrived back at Heathrow to the massed screams of hundreds of fans who had waited for hours for their return. All the papers carried accounts of girls screaming, crying, fainting and hurling themselves at barriers of policemen just for a glimpse of these gods.

The Beatles were a bit bewildered by it all. By this stage, bolstered by the hardships of Hamburg and elsewhere, they had built a tough exterior. They had no illusions that they were the perfect, lovable mop-tops of recent legend. They were in no position to make or break myths. It was all beyond their control now.

They treated interviews as a joke, and the repartee built up during months on the road came in to play, charming the journalists who had expected either star snootiness or muttered monosyllables from pampered thickos. The Beatles sparred with wit and intelligence. They wore the image of sharp, working-class kids made good. But despite their show of friendliness, there was a distance, an aloofness determined by their refusal to take success seriously that created a mystique. The clubbishness of the group kept them apart and gave them an unapproachability that at the same time created a desire among outsiders to be included but a sense that that could never be. The Beatles became instant aristocracy, a national institution.

3 Band on the Run

John, Paul, George and Ringo were at the centre of a vortex. By the end of 1963 The Beatles were living a completely unreal life. They were London based — John and Cynthia had found a flat in Kensington, as had Ringo and George. Paul had met Jane Asher, a young actress and daughter of psychiatrist Sir Richard Asher. She was smart, intelligent and on the verge of her own successful career. The relationship developed and before long Paul had moved into the Ashers' family home.

They scarcely dared set foot outside their homes for fear of being mobbed. So, when they weren't touring, they spent time with a small circle of friends drawn from the world of showbiz. They spent more and more time touring, and days became lost in a rush from hotel to theatre, back to the hotel, and on to the next venue. Life took on a rarefied quality. The world outside became something they remembered from the past. They were prisoners, and remained so for another two years at least.

Beatlemania was raging outside the walls. The hysteria was localised, confined to physical appearances by members of The Beatles, but to read the national press would suggest that the nation's adolescents were in a permanent state of frenzy. Pubescent girls screamed until they wet themselves and generally went into a lather. Psychologists in the posh Sundays talked of The Beatles acting as a sexual outlet for female fans; ministers of religion and even the editor of the *New Statesman* railed against the apparent mindlessness of The Beatle maniacs.

But the fact remains that these frenzied scenes were largely self-induced by girls who allowed the sight of The Beatles to trigger off a hysterical response. Jazz singer and writer George

39

Melly recalls two girls behind him at a Beatle concert discussing whether or not to scream at the support group or save their emotions for The Beatles. So, it was a conscious, or semi-conscious, process that many fans went through; it was a form of self-expression.

It comes down to the fact that The Beatles were more than just stars. The role their fans gave them was far more significant. Elvis had been a hero, a leader figure — someone to identify with, at least as a pose. But Elvis had limitations — he only *looked* rebellious. Verbally, he was slow and hamstrung. The Beatles were more tricksy altogether, as the press soon found out.

At first, the newspapers concentrated on the effects of Beatlemania. Then, when journalists got to talk to the foursome, they found something extra. The non-conformist edge to their gags came through as clear and fresh — especially in the wake of the ponderous, evasive statements from politicians during the Profumo affair. The public loved it. Here was the voice of normality — nice, local lads.

Had they just been local lads, they would never have triggered off the response that followed their every gesture. It is, of course, impossible to pin down just what made The Beatles great and their impact even greater. But there are clues.

The Beatles were more than the sum total of four personalities. What became known to the fans as 'The Beatles' was a complex of fact, observation, myth and daydream. First the facts. They all four came from relatively humble beginnings in Liverpool; two of them, Lennon and McCartney, were very talented indeed both as song-writers and musicians. Also, as a band, they were capable of vigorous and original, if occasionally rudimentary, music. Through the long nights of Hamburg and the bread and butter gigging on Merseyside, they had developed an unusually lively and informal stage act, through which their personalities shone. They had a certain style and they looked good on and off stage.

Observation: The kids saw that The Beatles were not far removed from them, in that they had sprung from Northern, urban surroundings with no great advantages in life. They observed that, far from being bull-dozed by the constant pressure of media attention, they managed to stay bright, natural and apparently unaffected by it. The Beatles, they noticed, did not try to lose their accents; in fact, they wore the Scouse like a badge. Far from apologising for their appearance, particularly their hair, they carried on in careless defiance of traditional British conservatism. Finally, the music, in the shape of Lennon's and McCartney's songs, spoke to *them*. The lyrics were full of 'me' and 'you' — easy to identify with. Yet, behind them, was a hint of rebellion.

Myth: Press coverage perpetrated the illusion of The Beatles as a foursome possessed of formidable wit, boundless charm and personalities which outshone those of normal mortals. Every joke was a killer, every aside a jewel. They were treated as down-market royalty, their every whim and action duly noted. They became a small elite of supermen who could do no wrong, cuddly supermen.

Daydream: These differed from boy to girl. Running the risk of sexism through generality, it could be said that the boys identified with The Beatles' style, elevation, musical ability and barbed wit. They also admired the way they forced the older generation to accept, even court, them, while at the same time being taken for a gentle ride. Their girl-pulling power was also a matter for deep respect. The girls saw them as a composite figure of their ideal hero: appreciative, kind, vulnerable, lordly, aggressive, virile and loveable.

At the height of Beatlemania, fans did not see The Beatles as their representatives so much as a fantasy extension of themselves. They provided in their minds two things that were progressively missing from their own lives: certainty and commitment. The Beatles seemed sure of themselves, confident of their own ability and purpose. With money, fame and talent, their lives seemed complete. For the youth of the 1960s such a certainty was a daydream. They were busy rejecting the values of their parents' generation. They wanted freedom from moral and material obligations yet they lacked purpose — they had no place to stand. The Beatles seemed to have cracked it. They appeared to have got to that ultimate hedonistic heaven where life became a daily round of unrestricted fun.

With a diminishing sense of social or spiritual purpose, young people had no cause to espouse, no battles to fight save that against adult authority, be it at school, work or home. Hero worship of The Beatles gave them the kind of commitment they were looking for. Here was something to

41

believe in that was not grey or regimented, that was not old and musty but visible, alive and exciting.

The hero worship spread across Britain to every corner of almost every social class. The Beatles were as much an established part of public school life as that of the grammar and secondary modern schools of the era. Later, when John Lennon noted 'We're more popular than Jesus now' (a comment that was hastily withdrawn), he said more than he knew. The Beatles were no person for person substitute, but the idea of Christianity as a living faith was certainly something that teenagers turned aside from.

By the end of 1963, at one extreme The Beatles were invited to play the Royal Command Performance, and were acclaimed by *The Times* music critic as 'The outstanding English composers of 1963'. At the other end of the scale, teenage schoolboys were being sent home by headmasters to return, shorn of their Beatle haircuts.

Such incidents are revealing. It has always been Britain's instinct to attempt to absorb and make respectable any potentially eccentric or rebellious elements in its culture. The arrival of The Beatles' institution was just such an instance. When The Beatles played for the Queen Mother and Princess Margaret, John charmed the audience with his impudence, quipping 'Will people in the cheaper seats clap your hands? All the rest of you, if you'll just rattle your jewellery . . .' It was a court jester's remark, but there was steel behind the surface innocence. They were not going to sell out completely.

William Mann's fawning tribute in *The Times* managed completely to miss the essential quality of the music. He referred, in lofty tones, to 'pandiatonic clusters' and 'Aeolian cadences' in a vain attempt to bring The Beatles music into line with some established pattern of recognised musical values. It still looks wrong.

In a sense, it was the headmasters, clinging to the importance of appearance as the vestige of the old accepted order, who better understood what The Beatles were about — that they stood *against* the status quo, not in the mainstream.

It is remarkable to consider what a change had come over The Beatles in one year. At the end of 1962, they had been ebullient and brash, but underneath, rather diffident — wondering whether they were really going to make it in the big city. Twelve months later, with four number one chart successes (all Lennon and McCartney songs) and two top-selling albums (their second, *With The Beatles,* had been released in November 1963), they were the nation's heart-throbs.

Yet, somehow, they took the change in status, the rapid acceleration of living pace, together with the constant media attention, all in their own stride. Manager Epstein had done much to keep them together and protect them, but it was the unity of The Beatles, inured to hardship and pressure, which enabled them to survive by playing so much of it as a joke and creating a shell around themselves so that nothing could break in. The ability of the four to shut out the outside world, the formation of an exclusive four-man club, contrived to enhance their appeal.

The next step for The Beatles was to conquer the United States, which no British pop artist had yet managed to do. The American record buying public were not interested in British rock'n'roll, or so said the record companies. Epstein had tried to convince Capitol in America, but they weren't interested in the four Beatles' singles, even though EMI, who owned Parlophone, also owned Capitol.

Epstein tried again with The Beatles' fifth single, 'I Want To Hold Your Hand', which had gone straight to number one in Britain in December and stayed there for five weeks. Capitol expressed cautious, pessimistic interest. But, as so often happens, the record buyers took a hand in things. Before Capitol had lifted a finger, just before Christmas 1963, the record was receiving air-play on small local stations by jocks who had contacts in Britain and who had got hold of British copies of the single. It started in Washington: the DJ kept playing the record and listeners pestered the station — where could they get the record? The news spread West and filtered back to Capitol. They began pressing copies at speed.

It had been the American audience who had discovered, even fostered, rock'n'roll. White American teenagers in the late Forties and early Fifties, bred with the crooners and the dance bands, looked elsewhere for authentic, exciting music. They discovered it on the black radio stations — rhythm and blues music. As enthusiasm grew, white musicians and blacks too began to modify the music, blending it with white country and developing what came to be known as rock'n'roll. But, as rock'n'roll developed, it too became flabby and soft as the commercial record machine tried to manufacture its own copies of such authentic rockers as Little Richard, Chuck Berry, Elvis Presley and Eddie Cochran. The music lost its way.

It was no wonder the Americans didn't take to British rock'n'roll, since it was mostly copies of the American copy. It had nothing new to say. The Beatles were different. They had discovered the original R&B artists and the original rockers for themselves. Their reaction was a different blend, something wholly new. But it *was* authentic and those early US fans realised it. At the same time, The Beatles were putting them back in touch with their roots, America's black music. Lennon said, 'We felt we had a message for America, which was "Listen to this music."'

They did. By mid-January 1964, 'I Want To Hold Your Hand' was number one in the US Top One Hundred. It was a definite first. The Beatles heard the news in Paris, where their egos were low having failed to excite Parisian fans who preferred the safer, more melodic fare provided by Trini Lopez. By the time Epstein broke the news, the single had sold one-and-a-half million copies. In no time, the American press were hot on their heels. As the British press had sought relief from Profumo and the Great Train Robbery, so the American press sought a lightening of the prevailing gloom from November 1963's tragic assassination of John F. Kennedy.

As news of the Mersey mop-tops floated across the Atlantic and plans were announced for a February visit, interest in the States grew rapidly. A crash promotion budget was set aside by Capitol. The Beatles were due to tour and to appear in the top-rating *Ed Sullivan Show*.

By dint of clever publicity manipulation, the already eager American fans were persuaded to welcome The Beatles at the airport. In the event, on February 7, 1964, five thousand of them hollered, cried and screamed as The Beatles stepped out of the plane. America, if anything, was more ready for The Beatles than Britain had been. The story was the same as at home, but the riots were bigger and the mobs more hysterical.

At their first American press conference, seasoned US journalists grilled these long-haired imports to the land of the crew cut. The Beatles, already adept at such sessions, flashed back with gags, and ironic put-downs that turned the questions on their heads. The press were baffled, but pleasantly surprised. The Beatles had cracked America.

To cap it all, while appearing to a seventy million strong audience on *The Ed Sullivan Show* on February 9, a telegram of congratulations was read out from John's and Paul's great hero, Elvis Presley. The tour was a sell-out, but again, the four of them were kept imprisoned for their own safety. All the while, a vast merchandising exercise for Beatle wigs, dolls and bags was mounted. On a subsequent tour, cans of Beatle breath were sold. One hotel cut the bed-linen used by The Beatles — unwashed — into small squares and sold each with a legal affidavit affirming that it had been slept on by a Beatle!

Even American evangelist Billy Graham had broken his strict rule and watched TV on Sunday to catch this phenomenon on *The Ed Sullivan Show*. His comment was not far from the mark: 'All are symptoms of the uncertainty of the times and the confusion about us.'

The British establishment wanted to get in on the act and, as usual, blew it. The Beatles were patronisingly invited to a British Embassy reception in Washington to announce the winners of the embassy raffle. They were harried by young diplomats who demanded co-operation and autographs and one woman tried to snip Ringo's hair with nail scissors. John left in disgust, and the group swore never to go near an embassy function again.

Back in Britain, their fame and the national obsession with The Beatles grew yet bigger. Their music became but a small part of the absurd preoccupation with their every move. They were touring constantly with hardly a break, but their concerts were a nonsense and they knew it. The moment they stepped on stage, hysteria broke loose. Gamely, they went through their paces but to no purpose. The music was drowned.

The only creativity left to them was in songwriting and recording. But, with no effort required to gain an audience, their playing suffered. Road manager Neil Aspinall had literally to push them on stage some nights — they hated it so much. Life for them was just a frenetic routine.

The press were still committed, spreading the idea of the clean, bright, working class heroes, loveable Beatles. There developed an accepted circle who saw that this status quo was maintained. But backstage and at the hotel, things were rather different. From the start of the British tours, The Beatles, captive as they were on this unreal merry-go-round from hotel to hotel, often not knowing what town and, later, what country they were in, sought distraction of any kind. By March, 1964, they were relying heavily on pep-pills to keep time with the furious pace of their lifestyle.

There were groupies by the score (though they were not called that then). Girls were sought and supplied at every stopping place. Lennon: 'The Beatles' tours were like the Fellini film *Satyricon* . . . if we couldn't get groupies, we would have whores and everything, whatever was going . . . When we hit town, we hit it . . . There's photographs of me crawling about in Amsterdam on my knees, coming out of whore houses . . . The police escorted me to the places, because they never wanted a big scandal, you see.'

The wild nights became part of the unreality. Ringo says it was the only fun they had. By their own admission they were like boy Caesars. Certainly, they found themselves with unlimited power and influence, but with little or no notion of what to do with it.

To add to the unreality, wherever they played, wheelchair patients would be pushed into their dressing rooms. The disabled young occupants were brought by their charges, presumably with the vain hope that some of The Beatles' god-like magic would rub off and heal them. In some cases, particularly in the States, they would be asked to touch the people. There is a hideous black humour about the absurdity of the practice, another clear indication that The Beatles, in the mind of some of the public, had transcended the mortal. The contrast is startling.

1964 continued, as one of the aides put it, to be 'One more stage, one more limo, one more run for your life'. There were odd breaks in the tours. John branched out with the publication in April of a patchy little book of doodles, poems and funnies, some dating back to his school exercise books. Called *John Lennon In His Own Write*, it received warm reviews from the quality press as a creative piece of anarchic goonery. Lennon was genuinely pleased at his literary success.

In the States, Beatle fans, courtesy of the record companies who rush-released their old singles, were now able to catch up on all The Beatles' songs to date. Their response meant that in one week in March, Beatles' records took up the first five places in the US Top One Hundred.

In July, there was the premiere of Dick Lester's imaginative first Beatle feature film, *A Hard Day's Night*. Recalling the pleasant side of Beatlemania, its shooting was a welcome break from yet another gruelling tour — this time of Scandinavia, Holland, the Far East and Australia.

In August, The Beatles returned to the States on a twenty-three city marathon tour. This time, they played only large sports arenas or convention centres and the group travelled, with their entourage, in a private plane. It was a crippling tour and the American fans were frightening. After each performance, The Beatles hurried direct from the stage to the waiting aircraft and on to the next city.

In between times The Beatles spent the money they were earning on clothes they never wore, trinkets and goods they never used. John bought Aunt Mimi a bungalow overlooking the harbour at Poole, in Dorset; Paul bought his father, now retired, a house on the Cheshire Wirral and a racehorse. John also bought himself a mock Tudor mansion in Weybridge, Surrey, but Paul bided his time, staying on with the Ashers until he found himself a large town house in St. John's Wood.

John found, to his dismay, that not far from his home, Fred Lennon was washing up in the kitchen of a hotel in Esher. Lennon senior chose his time to re-emerge, selling his life story to *Tit-bits* and *Weekend* magazines. He even brought out a record — 'That's My Life'. John said, 'I didn't want to see him. I was too upset about what he'd done to me and to my mother and that he should turn up when I was rich and famous and not bother turning up before. So I wasn't going to see him but he sort of blackmailed me in the press by saying all this about being a poor man washing dishes while I was living in luxury. I fell for it and saw him and we had some kind of relationship.' John gave him a flat and a small pension. Fred Lennon died a few years later of cancer.

Excess breeds boredom and the craving for new excitement. It was with already jaded palates that The Beatles began experimenting with drugs. They had always used them for the expedient of staying awake and on top. Now, they tried them for sensation. Pills came first, in different colours and varieties, uppers and downers. Marijuana came next. The excitement of rolling joints, inhaling and passing them on became a sort of élite, illicit communion. West Indians in the slum tenements of London had introduced the drug to the country. They smoked to help forget the squalor and degradation. The Beatles smoked to ease themselves, to forget the absurdities of the life created by and for them. *Help*, The Beatles' second film, was shot in a haze of dope.

Paul was surviving the onslaught. His residual toughness and exterior charm got him by. In his relationships with Jane Asher and her family, he had a semblance of normality to return to off tour. He was the one Beatle whose address remained secret from the fans, so he was able to be just that bit more free. Jane Asher was a good foil for him, too. She was independent and had her own successful career. She met McCartney as an equal and he respected her.

John, on the other hand, was going down slowly. For a while, he was content to stay at home between tours and play with Julian. But already, his relationship with Cyn was becoming a habit — all but forgotten when he was away. Cynthia Lennon had no illusions about being an equal partner with John; she resigned herself to her relegation to the background of his life. She accompanied him when she could but it was John who called the tune. But Lennon was unhappy. He let himself go and grew fat.

Around this time, he discovered a new musical influence, but had not quite absorbed it yet. He had heard the compelling whine of New York's rising poet and singer, Bob Dylan. Lennon would sit at home fiddling with his guitar, doodling and listening to Dylan.

The Beatles' chart-topping singles of 1964 showed that the song-writing team were not standing still. Throughout 1963, their singles had been neat and well tailored to the audience. But the lyrics were, at best, banal. But, by 1964, the wit, the sharpness with which they delivered their verbal lines was beginning to make itself audible in the songs with such phrases as 'A Hard Day's Night'.

Perhaps the fact that touring required so little of their musical energies meant that they were able to bring more attention to bear on the songs. Their first hit of 1964 — 'Can't Buy Me Love' — was more or less in line with the previous compositions. But their songwriting grew in assurance as the year progressed.

In 1964, pop songs remained only vague expressions of feeling — the lyrics provided a useful catch phrase here and there, but were more a vehicle for voice than meaning. But the music was improving: the melody lines, the sense of rhythm and pace was altogether sharper. Again, 'A Hard Day's Night' marked the change. The variations of tempo and direction in the song are masterly.

The songs of John and Paul were helped considerably by the improvement in recording equipment and techniques available to producer George Martin. He could now build up songs by superimposing layers of sound. Their third album, *Beatles For Sale,* is crammed with quality songs by Lennon and McCartney. The Beatles, if they hadn't before, were producing classy music.

1965 was the year of the Mods. They had actually been around for a year or two but, by 1965, they had come of age. The Mods were a largely working-class group of teenagers whose preoccupation was with fashion and style. They promoted the cult of the young. Being young was what gave life meaning. No self-respecting Mod would spend less than half his weekly earnings on clothes, went the legend. Their music was black soul and white R&B. The quintessential rock groups were The Who and The Small Faces.

The Mods created a new sense of high style for young Britons. Among the leaders of this new style were boutique owner John Stephen and designer Mary Quant. Simultaneously, they forced the fashion pace and supplied youth's demand for new ideas. London's Carnaby Street grew into a shrine to which all the fashion conscious flocked. Hipster trousers appeared, bright paisley ties, the mini skirt, the straight, ironed hair. London was beginning to swing.

The Beatles became part of the Carnaby Street package, keeping ahead of both fashions and drugs. The purple heart was the pep-pill of the moment, but The Beatles were into marijuana and, by early 1965, something a lot more powerful.

The story has been told and re-told about how George Harrison, his girlfriend, Patti Boyd, John and Cynthia Lennon went to a dinner party. After they'd eaten, coffee was served. In each cup was placed a solitary lump of sugar. Cynthia Lennon said, 'It was as if we suddenly found ourselves in the middle of a horror film.' Their host, without saying anything, had dipped the sugar into a drug called LSD. The four of them suffered four of them suffered delusions and paranoia and it took them three days to get over the experience. Lennon, however, was fascinated by what the drug did to the mind. Later, he tried it again and again and again . . .

But he was still down. He lived life in a haze of marijuana. He had the power to do anything, but was trapped into a machine that seemed to be running out of control. Overweight and depressed, Lennon wrote a plea. 'When ''Help'' came out in 1965, I was actually crying out for help. Most people think it's just a fast rock'n'roll song. I didn't realise it at the time because I was commissioned to write it for a movie. But later, I knew I was really crying out for help. It was my fat Elvis period . . . I was fat and depressed and I *was* crying out for help.'

> 'When I was younger, so much younger than today,
> I never needed anybody's help in any way,
> But now these days are gone, I'm not so self-assured
> Now I find I've changed my mind, I've opened up the doors.'

That particular song marked a significant stage in Lennon's development as a writer. Prior to this The Beatles' songs, almost all pop songs, had been concerned with self-expression only in the sense that the music itself was expressive. Here, Lennon was beginning, albeit semi-consciously at this stage, to articulate his feelings in words. It was a trend that was to continue.

In spring 1965, as is standard practice, people on the Queen's birthday honours lists were sounded out by Buckingham Palace as to whether they would accept the honour. The Beatles were told that Harold Wilson's new Labour government (he had been voted in in 1964) were offering them the MBE. Lennon's first reaction was to say no; he thought it hypocritical to take such an award. But Brian insisted that it was only right to accept. On June 12, the honours were announced and a minor storm of protest followed. Some similarly honoured folk returned their medals in disgust.

Picking up their MBE's was a matter of playing the game and they played it with much gravity — even buying bowler hats for the occasion. So the story goes, they smoked a quick joint in the palace washroom before going through their paces for the Queen!

The singles continued;. 'Day Tripper', 'Help', 'Yesterday' and

'We Can Work It Out'. 'Yesterday' was seen as a break-through. In fact it was not a Beatles record at all — just Paul on acoustic guitar and strings. Paul had let the most sentimental part of his songwriting character show. If 'Help' had been John's solo effort of the year, Paul's answer was decidedly more limp but also much more universally popular. The Beatles' last single of 1965 marked a change of pattern too: they dispensed with the old idea of the 'A'-side with a filler song on the back. They now put out double 'A'-side singles, knowing that whichever side got played, it would still sell the record.

Their second film *Help,* another Dick Lester caper — strong on knockabout humour and light in all other departments but music — was released and swallowed up by the fans. The soundtrack album provided another selection of Lennon and McCartney songs which showed once more how they had matured. 'You've Got To Hide Your Love Away' showed the results of Lennon's attentions to Bob Dylan.

However, their appearances at premieres, the MBE award ceremony, the publication of Lennon's second book, *A Spaniard In The Works,* were the few highlights in the year. Still they spent the rest of the time touring, touring, touring. On one such US tour in August 1965, they played Shea Stadium to 55,000 people with gross receipts of £304,000.

By the end of the year, The Beatles were determined to stop touring. Though it was never announced as such, they embarked on their last ever tour of Britain in December, 1965.

1966 was much the same as the year before, except that after August 29 they toured no more. It was special in that it was a year of lasts: for the last time as a group they visited France, Italy, Spain, Hamburg (where they were received as long-lost sons), Tokyo and Manila (where they accidentally snubbed President Marcos' wife and had to leave).

Their fourth and final tour of the USA began in August, under a cloud. There were stories of the burning of Beatles records and effigies throughout the Southern Bible Belt. A section of fundamentalist southern clergy got very hot under the collar and The Beatles were banned on thirty-five radio stations.

The tide of anger arose from some lately published remarks by John Lennon. In March, 1966, in an interview with Maureen Cleave of the *Evening Standard,* he had said, 'Christianity will go. It will vanish and shrink. I needn't argue about that. I'm right and I will be proved right. We are more popular than Jesus now. I don't know which will go first — rock'n'roll or Christianity. Jesus was all right but his disciples were thick and ordinary. It's them twisting it that ruins it for me.'

In fact, he had been reading Hugh J. Schonfield's book *Passover Plot*, which attached selfish reasons to the disciples' spreading of Christianity. He had regurgitated it, undigested, and its ramifications, though belated, were fierce. The reaction shook John, who blamed himself only for not choosing his words more carefully. At the start of the tour, Lennon announced to a press conference, 'I'm not anti-God, anti-Christ or anti-religion. I wouldn't knock it. I didn't mean we were greater or better.' The offended elements, greatly appeased, settled down and the tour went on. But it put a crack in the image of The Beatles as four regular guys. Even so, American people still continued to bring blind, crippled and deformed children to their dressing room. Lennon recalled: 'This boy's mother would say, "Go on, kiss him, maybe you'll bring back his sight."'

The tour was a bad one for The Beatles. A clairvoyant had predicted that they would die in a plane crash. There were still demos and enough electricity in the air to make them fear that some madman might be out there with a gun. . .

In June, in Britain, The Beatles' first ever non-lovesong had failed to reach the number one spot at one leap. A week later it was there, but had the Lennon and McCartney team micalculated? The double 'A'-side, 'Paperback Writer'/'Rain', was just a little too clever. Paul had written 'Paperback Writer' and John 'Rain'. Influenced by The Byrds and Bob Dylan (who they had met and smoked with on more than one back-stage occasion), the single marked one more stage in the writer's history. They were still commercially accessible but they became more and more concerned with content.

In August, a second single was released, 'Eleanor Rigby'/ 'Yellow Submarine'. The poetic narrative, together with further experimentation with strings on Paul's 'Eleanor Rigby' and the imaginative collage of sound on 'Yellow Submarine' heralded the fact that Lennon and McCartney were no longer the purveyors of slick, vacuous, commercial pop. There had been signs in the previous album *Rubber Soul*, but here they displayed a high degree of creativity.

52

Revolver, the album which followed, in its underplayed black and white sleeve (designed by old Hamburg buddy, Klaus Voorman, who had since joined Manfred Mann as bass player) was a warren of creative activity. The music was a mixture of the complex and the simple. McCartney had gone poetic and Lennon had gone surreal. Their lyrics were now a match for the music. They had always managed to marry the two before but, on *Revolver,* the combination suddenly entered a different league. It was art, not rarefied museum material, but genuine mass-media art.

On August 29, 1966 at Candlestick Park, San Francisco, The Beatles gave their last live appearance anywhere in the world. There was no official statement to that effect but rumour grew, became confused and led to the fear that they were actually splitting up. Eventually, the news was made public. The Beatles would not tour again.

The main reason given was that their music had become so complex, involving the use of orchestras and electronic technology, that they were no longer in a position to reproduce it on stage. But the real reason has already been stated: they could no longer face living on the run in a mobile prison of their own making. Musically, the whole operation was a farce; they had become a glorified zoo act and they were sick of it.

So, August 29, 1966, saw the end of a Beatles era. The years 1963 to 1966 were a remarkable period of intensity and startling development. The quality and marked progression of The Beatles' music over those four years alone refute the arguments of those who thought they were the product of media manufacture.

They had begun as pop singers, peddling catch lines and rhythmic melodies. By 1965, they were warning America they would not play segregated audiences: 'We feel strongly about civil rights.' By 1966, hair grown out, their music Dylanized, they began to appear less as pop stars than leaders. Dissidence in the ranks of youth was growing. The rebellious young were now looking to The Beatles for words of wisdom. John Lennon and Paul McCartney were now songwriters with something to say. They had helped pull pop music into a new area where ideas could be discussed, where it could be more than chart material. It was no mean achievement for patchily educated, untrained musicians who, with touring behind them, now looked forward to enjoying their creativity at leisure.

4 Only Northern Songs?

John Lennon and Paul McCartney began writing songs together in the late 1950s. They wrote hundreds — filled exercise books with them. They were simple, almost banal songs of the 'Love Me Do' type with only the vaguest doh, ray, me references to give a clue as to the tune. Slowly, as their ambitions grew, they began to write 'Another Lennon-McCartney Original' at the top of the scribbled lyric sheets. Inspired by the then current big writers of the Sixties hits, they said: 'We wanted to be the Goffin and King of England'. Who would have known then that focusing on such a target would be setting their sights too low?

They were not writing songs in a vacuum. They were Liverpudlians. Liverpool was always a city with a particular flavour. Lennon recalled it in later life. 'It was going poor, a very poor city and tough. But people have a sense of humour because they are in so much pain, so they are always cracking jokes. They are very witty, and it's an Irish place. It's where the Irish came when they ran out of potatoes, and it is where black people were left, or worked as slaves, or whatever.

'It's cosmopolitan, and it's where the sailors would come home with blues records from the Americans on the ships. There is the biggest country and western following in England in Liverpool, besides London — always besides London, because there is more of it there.'

Lennon said, 'We were like the new kids coming out.' He and Paul had unconsciously soaked up the atmosphere of their city background, which included the indigenous sense of wit and, by the time they were teenagers, the sounds of rhythm and blues and rock'n'roll. Just as humour was the Scouse defence against adversity, so music was Lennon's and McCartney's escape from, not so much pain — though Lennon claims to have felt it acutely all his life — but more from the regimented expectations of school, career and drudgery.

Wisely, when they began recording in 1963, they elected to ditch all their old material. This instinct led them to write as they went along, reacting to their rapidly changing lives as fame caught them up in a whirl of frenzied movement. From 'Please, Please Me' on, they wrote together on the road.

In this period, as they wrote on tour buses, backstage and in hotel rooms, they wrote more directly together than at any other time. The two would sit with their guitars near enough to hear what each other was playing but far enough away to concentrate on their own sequence of chords. Separately, they would chug away, trying out melody lines and chord changes until one would suddenly take an interest in the embryonic tune emerging from the other. When one realised the other had got that indefinable something, they would join forces — pushing the melody, making changes and putting odd phrases to the emerging tune.

This was how almost all their early hits, such as 'From Me To You' and 'I Want To Hold Your Hand', were written. Their ideas were simpler then, and they wrote less with records in mind than the live audiences they were playing to. They were looking for instant, visible fan reaction.

They say that the songs became better as they became more adept at putting them together and as they improved as musicians. As they grew in confidence and expertise, Lennon and McCartney threw in sharper lines, using the music with more imagination. Still the songs were about love gained, lost, unrequited. It never occurred to them that pop music could be about anything else. All the same, it remained fresh and original.

Inevitably, their characters influenced the way they wrote. John was the cynic, the tough rock'n'roller; Paul was the man for instant cute melody, the soft touch. While this remained true in a general sense, John showed on more than one occasion that he had a gift for tenderness and Paul that he was equally capable of rumbustious rock'n'roll. But the songs that could be pinned, more or less, on one composer did not emerge until later — around the time of the third or fourth albums.

For a long time, they were not conscious about having to say anything through their songs. What they had to say came through in their stance, their general image as non-conformists. It came through as a matter of feel. Before the days of 'Revolution' and 'Give Peace A Chance', someone asked Lennon if he'd ever written an anti-war song. 'All our songs are anti-war songs,' he replied. The songs were impressionistic, unchallenging, but they took their place in a growing youth sub-culture that, if not resolutely anti-establishment, was at least implicitly anti-authority.

The Beatles' music was electric, mass-media folk music. When William Mann in *The Times* at the end of 1963 tried to give The Beatles a place in music history, he missed the point because he saw them in an 'art' context. Lennon and McCartney had no such intentions. Their music was part of a dialogue with their audience. Essentially topical, it communicated the experience of living *now*.

The fact that they were communicating to millions rather than to a handful of pseudo-ethnics in a cellar folk club, meant simply that they were getting to the grass roots quicker and more effectively. This was crucial, because it was the radio, record player and TV that had everything to do with the development of the growing youth culture. Precisely because the media was mass, teenagers throughout Britain and America were developing a shared experience. The factors that were influencing London kids — the songs, the TV shows and interviews — were the same ones working on those in Cardiff or Glasgow.

As Lennon and McCartney developed as people, as they went through new experiences, so this came out in their music and fans picked up on it. But it was not simply a matter of The Beatles influencing youth; it was nowhere as direct as that. Lennon and McCartney's songs were part of a larger process. The songwriters themselves belonged to a changing world. The events and feelings of the age changed them, as it was changing their audience. In some ways, the music they wrote was a reflection of what was going on around them. In that way, their audience informed them. On the other hand, Lennon and McCartney were by nature quick to pick up on moods, fashions and attitudes and these they communicated, through their songs and lives, to the public. In that way, they were leaders and catalysts for change.

Because they were admired, because young people identified with them, for want of any other social or spiritual direction, they aped their idols. Consequently, the fact that The Beatles caught on to Sixties fashion changes in clothes and hair style meant a ripple effect among their audience on both sides of the Atlantic. The same thing happened with drugs and attitudes towards sex, politics and religion. The songs played their part, even though, as John said, 'People think The Beatles know what's going on. We don't. We're just doing it.' But 'just doing it' was enough for their fans. They wanted a piece of the action too.

By late 1964-65, Lennon and McCartney were more conscious of what they were writing about. Bob Dylan's influence among musicians was so big that it was hard to compete. His relationship with The Beatles was not a close one. They had met, but the meeting of their music was the more important. To Dylan, The Beatles showed that rock'n'roll need not be commercial pop. The vibrancy of Lennon's and McCartney's songs made a profound impression on him.

Dylan recalls, 'They were doing things nobody else was doing. Their chords were outrageous, just outrageous, and their harmonies made it all valid. I knew they were pointing the direction of where music had to go. I was not about to put up with other musicians, but in my head The Beatles were it.' It was some time before Bob Dylan electrified his music — he was still a folkie then — but he always remembered the stunning effect The Beatles had on him.

Lennon gives credit in reverse to Dylan. 'I started thinking about my own emotions — I don't know when exactly it started, like, 'I'm A Loser' or 'Hide Your Love Away' or these kind of things. Instead of projecting myself into a situation, I would try to express what I felt about myself, which I've done in my books. I think it was Dylan who helped me realise that — not by any discussion or anything, but just by hearing his work. I had a sort of professional songwriter's attitude to writing pop songs; we would turn out a certain style of song for a single and we would do a certain style of thing for this, that and the other thing. I was already a stylised songwriter on the first album. But to express myself I would write *Spaniard In The Works* or *In His Own Write,* the personal stories which were expressive of my personal emotions. I'd have a separate songwriting John

Lennon who wrote songs for the sort of meat market and I didn't consider them — the lyrics or anything — to have any depth at all. They were just a joke. Then I started being me about songs, not writing them objectively, but subjectively.'

Dylan showed him, and McCartney too, that rock'n'roll could be a medium for geuine feeelings and content. Lennon remembered such songs as 'In My Life', 'Help' and 'Girl' as songs he had special feelings for because 'they're all personal records . . . they were the ones I really wrote from experience.' As time wore on, for John these songs came with increasing frequency — songs where the lyrics came first and were set to a tune. These he offered up all but complete. Still Lennon and McCartney wrote together, but with a new dimension of possibilities of imagery and meaning open to them.

From 1965 through to the autumn of 1966, The Beatles were still touring and consequently John and Paul were still thrust together for long periods, sharing a great deal in songwriting. That sharing was essential to the quality of their music. Despite the fact that the caricature of Lennon and McCartney's separate contributions is too superficial, Lennon *was* harsh and self-indulgent and needed some edges of his songwriting smoothed down. McCartney, left to *his* own devices, did tend to wax sentimental. When their relationship became strained towards the end of The Beatles' career as a band, this problem emerged most visibly.

John's song, 'The Ballad Of John And Yoko', released as a single in 1969, was written alone and, in fact, was all-but recorded alone, Paul coming in to play bass and drums. The song recounts his marriage to Yoko and the honeymoon bed-in for peace at the Amsterdam Hilton. John was at his most paranoid and defensive: 'Christ, you know it ain't easy/you know how hard it can be/the way things are going/they're going to crucify me.' It bore the hallmarks of Lennon at his best and his worst. On the other hand it was good, solid rock'n'roll — positive and gutsy. Lennon's voice is strong — he always had one of the best voices in the business. But the song is so indulgently chip-on-the-shoulder, that it's almost painful. In better times, Paul would have eased him out of the sulks, or at least made the end result less mordant.

'The Long Winding Road' from *Let It Be,* was Paul's solo effort. Though recorded with the rest of The Beatles and, without McCartney's consent, re-mixed and overdubbed with violins, horns and choir, by producer Phil Spector, it was the sentiments of Paul alone. A mawkish, sentimental dirge, it was, nevertheless, a lovely melody. But, with such lyrics as 'The wild and windy night that the rain washed away/has left a pool of tears crying for the day', it became a saccharin weepy. John would never have let him get away with it.

George Martin knew their abilities only too well. He regarded Paul as the most complete musician, a kind of one-man Rodgers and Hart. He was able, at the drop of a hat, to produce an attractive, commercial melody with words to match. Martin also noted that John's natural talent with words spurred him on to make better, more rounded songs with a firmer edge.

On the other hand, he said, John was lazy. While Paul constantly needed an audience to hear and appreciate his music, John wrote for his own amusement. It took McCartney's keenness and energy to complete his fragments of songs, to package them. Thus, collectively, they managed to write the most impressive body of rock songs ever.

From late 1966 to early 1968, their songwriting procedure changed. John and Paul would work alone, in the demo studios in their respective houses. Paul would work on complete songs, finding the tune first and then sketching in lyrics. These items he kept in his head ready for when he and John met. John would work out fragments — a line here, a chord change there, writing down or memorising the lyrics that seemed to pop into his head.

When the two got together, often with others around proffering suggestions, they would work in an apparently scatter-brained fashion, Paul on the piano, breaking into old Beatles' numbers or current hits of the day. At surreal or foolish suggestions from one or the other, they would fall about laughing. All the while, the collective Lennon-McCartney unconscious would work and they would fill in the holes or buttress the weak points in the original schemes. A fair number of songs would come quickly, by virtue of either Paul or John having a more or less complete idea of where the song was going. But often, the songs had to be created out of thin air.

'About a third of our songs are pure slog', Paul observed. Come the time to record a new album, they would find that, between them, they had enough material for two-thirds of the final product. Then, they would have to sit down, starting around 2 pm, and give themselves the rest of the day to produce a song. In this workman-like fashion, they would continue until the quota was complete. Even with this process, the songs were rarely finished products when they reached the studios, the last verse often being written by an informal committee of Beatles. Paul claims that few of their songs were inspired.

As it happens, few songs ever are, at least in any direct, bolt-from-the-blue sense. Lennon and McCartney's songs were culled from a variety of sources. They were manufactured from snatches of conversation, lines of verse, newspaper reports, hoardings, shop signs, observation, feelings and genuine perceptive insight. It seems they rarely wrote as a reaction to immediate surroundings, but from a collection of memories. For instance, 'Penny Lane' and 'Strawberry Fields' — both songs about areas of Liverpool — were written long after Paul and John had left the 'Pool. Both used the time of reflection spent in the Indian retreat of the Maharishi to write prolifically, though not about India or the Maharishi: they wrote material for the double set that came to be known as *The White Album*.

Drugs played a part in their writing. They were smoking marijuana regularly from the time of *Help*, and John, in particular, was taking LSD with crazy regularity from 1965 onwards. There is no doubt that much of the imagery of *Sergeant Pepper* came out of drug experiences, but few songs were actually about the *taking* of drugs. Perhaps one of the most positively acid-oriented songs was 'She Said She Said', from *Revolver*. Largely a John Lennon creation, it arose out of the first occasion Lennon dropped acid intentionally, in California, in 1965. 'She said I know what it's like to be dead, I know what it is to be sad/and she's making me feel like I've never been born.' The nightmare images are those of a mind jacked up by artificial stimulants.

It's tempting to think that the genius of Lennon and McCartney needed this kind of outside prodding, that LSD could give them a vision impossible by other routes. But that's a delusion. They took drugs because they met people who were into them already and because, despite their fame and success, they still felt empty. Exploring new worlds was part of the process of trying to find themselves, of trying to come to terms with themselves and the world around them. Ultimately, it led them nowhere.

As it was, the amount of creative talent between them was more than sufficient to provide great rock music. It needed only their own wills to unlock it. But Lennon and McCartney were only normal people with normal shortcomings and normal vulnerabilities, living under *abnormal* pressures. They were human. Lost in this world, as most people are, they reacted accordingly.

Lennon and McCartney, as has been said, were very different characters. That difference provided a creative clash of mind and vision which, as long as The Beatles remained as an entity, produced positive sparks — 'Please, Please Me', 'Hard Day's Night', 'I Feel Fine', 'Ticket To Ride', 'Eleanor Rigby', 'Strawberry Fields', 'A Day In The Life'. What more could we ask?

5 Fixing a Hole

When The Beatles quit touring at the end of the summer of 1966, some people thought it would be the end of The Beatles themselves. In a sense, it was — at least the beginning of the end. Even though *Sergeant Pepper*, their ultimate achievement, and three more albums were to appear, The Beatles' retreat to their separate haunts marked the end of an era. It also marked the beginning of the final act of the drama.

During the years of Beatlemania, with its non-stop touring, the unrelenting pressure of fans and press and the constant mobility, The Beatles leant on each other in order to retain their sanity. Their manager and aides helped form a protective shell, inside of which they were trapped. It meant that they had no real individual existence outside of The Beatles. Naturally, there were dynamics within the group. John and Paul were particularly close because they were the working partnership. They provided the initiative, the impetus on which The Beatles relied for their continuing existence and success. But collectively, all their energies were fed into being Beatles. Although the pressure had not always been so great, they had lived as Beatles for almost six years.

When they came home from the final tour of the USA, their desire was not so much to branch out as individuals but simply to leave behind the constant grind of meaningless public performances. They did not strategise for the future at all. They just stopped.

Having returned home, George, John and Ringo to their Surrey abodes and Paul to his newly bought St John's Wood house, they then had time to consider. George, perhaps the one least happy as a Beatle, developed his growing interest in the sitar and Indian music and culture generally, a course that was to lead him — and for a while the others — to mysticism. Ringo played with his expensive toys and various small-time business ventures.

The focus falls inevitably on Lennon and McCartney. How would these two very different characters operate without the force of circumstance — always in each other's company, always in search of something to do to stave off the boredom of yet another hotel suite? The question is already partly answered in the previous chapter: their approach was adapted and, naturally, their songs became more individualistic. But they found they still needed one another, still needed the spur of the other.

In fact, The Beatles still all felt the need to be together, even if the gaps between their meetings grew longer. The unit, the companionship built up over the years, was so strong that they could not do without each other. Wives and girlfriends were still secondary. Who else understood them? Who else had been through the same fantasy nightmare unreality that they had? No one.

Meeting together after breaks of weeks or months, they would stand around awkwardly, as if at a formal reunion. Sometimes they would shake hands; at other times they would leap about uttering looney cries or hug each other. Later, as the mystic urge became strong, they would just hold each other in silence. There was a reassurance there — a completeness they could not find elsewhere.

Back at home, things were different. Alone with their thoughts, they began to realise that there must be life after The Beatles. For John, there was no immediate problem. He had been asked to play the part of Private Gripweed in a Dick Lester film, *How I Won the War*. The many-faceted Lennon coped admirably but was not enamoured with acting or actors. He appeared in the film — to critical approval — as a World War II tommy, complete with National Health specs.

John had always been very short-sighted, but such was his image consciousness that he had refused to wear them in public. Perhaps, because stage appearances were over and he had time to reflect, he could now be more honest with himself, and took to wearing glasses again. He opted for the owlish style he had worn in the movie. They became an essential part of the much photographed Lennon, whose public persona took on a new aspect from then on.

Paul had no immediate project into which to throw his boundless energies, so he decided to improve himself. Being a Beatle had taken up all his time and he was keen to make up. London in the Sixties was a melting pot of new art, theatre and music. Paul told the press he had 'to know what people are doing'. He was helped by Jane Asher, who provided an entrée into this exciting new world. The press were less interested in McCartney's cultural pursuits than in speculating about when and if he and the successful young actress were to become engaged.

Paul's musical talents were not allowed to lie fallow. He composed the theme music for a British film comedy, *The Family Way,* providing a neat and melodic score. But more than the others, Paul missed touring. He needed an audience — even when he was writing songs. He would play his half-finished pieces over to friends and acquaintances, not for criticism, but for approval and reaction. He had been the last to decide that the touring should stop and the first to want to get back to it.

Always the keeny in the earlier Beatle days, Paul did most in the post-touring period to keep The Beatles alive as an entity, suggesting ideas and initiating meetings. His house in Cavendish Avenue was close to the EMI studios at Abbey Road and it became a stop-off base for all the others before recording. He and John finished many songs in the top floor studio.

Brian Epstein, meantime, began a slow slide from which he never recovered. His personal life continued to be a mess. Fame and fortune for The Beatles had brought a reflected glory on himself. He was fêted and lionised but never quite received the credit and celebrity he secretly hoped for. He continued to make disastrous rough trade assignations and was badly beaten up on a number of occasions. Aides bailed him out of several tricky blackmail cases where former boyfriends would turn nasty and threaten to reveal his story to the press.

But Epstein pressed on. His stable of artists had grown and his business ventures multiplied. A mixture of flair, shrewdness, honesty and naïvety, he never quite capitalised on his assets — not even The Beatles. For a long time, he never really understood how much they were worth. But his personal devotion to their well-being was total. He was the complete

Mother Hen, clucking around his charges, making sure they had everything they wanted — protection from the press, the fans and the mercenaries.

He was at this best when they were on tour. It was his job to make sure everything went smoothly and The Beatles took him for granted. There was a close bond between them and they gave him credit for what he'd done, but always saw him as the man in the suit — the necessary buttress between them and the establishment. After the earliest days, when he had prepared lengthy memos on dress and behaviour and given them lists of songs to play, he was wise enough to leave musical decisions to the foursome and George Martin. Only once did he make so bold as to offer a suggestion. The Beatles were recording and John was singing lead. Brian, from the control booth, switched on the studio intercom: 'I don't think that sounded quite right, John.' 'You stick to your percentages, Brian. We'll look after the music,' came the icy, devastating reply. It hurt him badly. Things had not gone well for him ever since The Beatles decided to stop touring. On tour, they needed Epstein as shepherd, go-between and fixer. Epstein needed to be needed and, when the performances stopped, he felt his usefulness was finished, too.

He drank heavily — mostly brandy — and took heavy doses of uppers and downers to get him through the days and nights. He couldn't sleep, so he dosed himself heavily; then he couldn't wake, so he would take another batch to get himself going. There were overdoses — accidental or otherwise — but he was rescued in time by staff and friends. From autumn 1966 until his death a year later, he saw less and less of his fantasy group.

For John, time lay heavy on his hands, but it was not too much of a burden. Never one of the world's workers, he was dictated to by impulse. Few of the many lushly carpeted rooms in his Weybridge house saw their owner. He spent most of his time in a small, cosy, lived-in room next to the kitchen. It had a large, sliding glass door overlooking the garden and swimming pool, and a clutter of ornaments, posters and photographs. Here he, Cynthia and Julian lived, neglecting the luxurious furniture of the other reception rooms. John would spend hours curled up on a too-small sofa or, on sunny days, sitting on the steps outside.

He would remain silent for hours in either place, staring at nothing in particular. He was dropping acid tabs frequently and regularly in this period. Always brooding and introspective,

LSD turned him even further into himself. His relationship with Cynthia became a habit — it was comfortable, but there was no spark. They were living more like brother and sister than husband and wife. He loved Julian, but his family were by no means the core of his life. It was still The Beatles that gave him focus and meaning, but, left to his own devices more and more, Lennon began, unconsciously, to search for something else. He now saw that his life was empty. John's re-awakened interest in the arts, his espousal of divergent and sometimes contradictory causes stem from this time.

At first, during the winter months of 1966, he would sleep in so late he never saw daylight. But, he thought, if he was doing nothing, he might as well be doing it when there was some sun around. So, inside or out, he would sit thumbing a book or magazine, then putting it aside again. The TV might catch his attention for a while. Then, back to contemplation. As night drew in, if there was nothing on — The Beatles had become frequenters of night clubs catering for the new pop aristocracy, such as Blases or Sybilla's — Lennon would retire to his studio and doodle, record snatches of new songs or tinker, late into the night. Cynthia and Julian would rise quietly next morning, leaving the master to sleep until midday or so. But, after November 1966, Lennon's contemplations were progressively disturbed by a small, black-haired figure . . .

Lennon, his mind drifting, engaged his imaginations in the art world once more. The late Sixties was a springtime for the avant garde, and John was often invited to private views at small galleries around London. One such gallery, the Indica, had been opened by Marianne Faithfull's husband, John Dunbar, an acquaintance of Lennon's. Dunbar invited him to the Indica to meet an artist busy hanging a new show of her own work. The show featured bits and pieces of esoteric nonsense which she placed around the gallery in high seriousness. There was a fresh apple with a sign saying £200. Lennon recounted how he climbed up a stepladder to a blank canvas attached to the ceiling. From the canvas hung a spyglass. Looking through it, he saw, in tiny letters, the word 'yes'. He was impressed by the ironic humour in the work and felt it was 'positive'.

John Dunbar introduced the artist. She was a small, strong-faced Japanese-American named Yoko Ono. Surprisingly, she didn't know who he was. She just handed him a card which said, 'Breathe'. He did, and left the show intrigued, but not smitten either by her or her work. He met her again at another show, and both stood off from the other out of shyness.

Yoko, a shrewd businesswoman, approached him to back one of her shows and he agreed. She gave him a copy of her book *Grapefruit,* full of one-line epithets, like 'Bleed' or 'Paint until you drop dead'. It amused him and irritated him at the same time. He kept it by the bed, and he and Cynthia would joke about its silliness and Lennon would curse its intellectual artiness. But it held a fatal fascination for him. Yoko Ono was fast becoming an important figure in his life, although he had yet to realise it.

The Beatles, infected by the slowed pace of their own lives and the lack of contact with one another, failed to come up with a sequel to the innovative *Revolver.* They settled instead for a package of oldies for the Christmas Beatle market. Songs were coming slower now, and the impetus to work together was less urgent.

However, Paul and John did complete one song for the non-existent new album. They were hardly Lennon and McCartney songs, but individual products of startling creativity that said a lot about their separate authors. Much longer than the average three-minute single of the accepted norm, they were nevertheless put out by Parlophone in February, 1967, as a double 'A'-side: 'Penny Lane'/'Strawberry Fields Forever'.

If Lennon and McCartney were not already established as songwriters of all-time class, these two songs put them among the greats. More than that, the musical concept was so sure, so imaginative, the final pieces so complete, that it took The Beatles and rock music into a new dimension. The songs had consumed as much money and time as many an album. They were carefully constructed, yet were made with a flair that took care of any pomposity.

'Penny Lane' was Paul's sprightly, nostalgic evocation of good times in Liverpool. Penny Lane is on the edge of the city centre, a familiar haunt of McCartney's. The backward vision is seen through drug-experienced eyes. It still looks bright but, now and then, it all appears 'very strange', as if in a dream. But always, it is a Paul kind of dream — sharp, bright colours and funny people. Despite its brightness and brittleness, a showcase of McCartney's wit and facility, there is something knowing about it, the Paul behind the music.

67

'Strawberry Fields' exhibits none of these surface qualities. It is a composition that contains the dark brooding vision of Lennon. It is significant that, at this stage in their careers — given time to reflect — both should produce personal songs about the city they grew up in. And how differently they saw their past.

Oddly enough, Strawberry Fields, a Salvation Army home which held a fête every summer, was somewhere John remembered with affection. Yet acid transformed Lennon's introspection with surreal reflections of his own childhood feelings of alienation, of being somehow different from everyone else. Listening to the song is to be drawn into one of those dreams where nothing quite connects, and where there is only a semblance of reality.

They both remain marvellous songs — as good as anything they have ever written — marking a point where poetry and music meshed together. Here were two adult people making music out of their own experiences. Paul coated his feelings with a surface charm that, by its brightness, showed it was a way of coping with what was going on inside him — a way of pushing back any hint of darkness. John, always the more transparent, let his feelings flood out.

It is tempting to analyse further, but piece-by-piece dissection ruins the impact of the songs themselves. All that need be said is that Lennon and McCartney revealed themselves as individuals still trying to come to terms with their world. In both cases, there was a sense that they were trying to compensate for the fact that they had not yet found themselves, and were writing about their past as a way of trying to make sense of it all — however unconscious those feelings were.

The singles helped win them a wider audience, who, intrigued by 'Eleanor Rigby' and the like, began to see The Beatles as artists more serious than the average pop star — artists who were dealing with *real* feelings and experiences. The student population, who had been taken into the field of folk-rock by the example of Bob Dylan who was now putting his tortured, poetic images to rock'n'roll, saw in The Beatles people who could speak for them also.

Meanwhile, the mass teenage audience were not all so sure. For the first time since 'Please, Please Me', a Beatles' single failed to make number one, missing by one place. But The Beatles' new direction continued.

As ever, The Beatles caught the mood of the times. 1967 was the year of flower power, of Haight Ashbury, of Monterey. The youth culture that had its beginnings in the muttered dissent of Fifties' teenagers, had grown more confident and vocal in the early Sixties, had seen the rise of an articulate, idealistic civil rights movement in the mid-Sixties, blossoming in the last third of the decade into a genuine alternative culture. It was an attempt by the dissident young to stake a claim for a society based on *their* values, rather than those of their parents' generation.

It was doomed from the start, since the attempt to retreat from the nasty world of western technocracy and capitalism was built on dreams and a belief that man, left to his own devices, and given a chance to be true to himself, would find his way to a peaceful co-existence with his brothers. The foundations were too shallow to take the weight of such dreams. Humans, being what they are, have a built-in tendency to failure when it comes to a perpetual state of love and peace. Not even regular doses of euphoric drugs could change the fabric of human nature. But the leaders of the hippy culture believed that it really could happen.

The Beatles half believed it, too. As far back as December, 1965, they had put out a single — largely written by a Paul full of optimistic sentiment. Ostensibly a lovesong, 'We Can Work It Out' ran: 'Life is very short, and there's no time/for fussing and fighting my friend'. In the flower-scented summer of love in 1967, they brought out a hippy anthem, 'All You Need Is Love', full of the human potential to get it all together. 'Nowhere you can be that isn't where you meant to be', it counselled. 'It's easy/All you need is love.'

It was a nice idea, but ironic that it came from a band who found it anything but easy to tolerate any but their own kind. Even the sharp-witted Lennon had set aside his cynicism in the fervour that infected the times. It *was* easy if you lived a life buttressed from the rigours of routine normality and could escape in a haze of dope from the real world.

The Beatles were listened to for their opinions, as well as their music, and their loving words touched a chord in those who felt there might just be a road away from the cant of the politicians and the deadening demands of materialism.

The hippy culture, with its sprawling experiments at making an alternative society, was a *genuine* attempt by alienated young people to come to terms with the contradictory world in which they found themselves. But their efforts were essentially diversionary. The feeling was that, if you could hold the pressures and problems of the world at arm's length, you could possibly get your head together enough to make a difference to the straight society simply by *being* different.

In a similar way, The Beatles' big project of the year was diversionary. It was their most imaginative and ambitious album ever. Written almost exclusively by Lennon and McCartney, *Sergeant Pepper's Lonely Hearts Club Band* still stands out as the most memorable album in the history of rock'n'roll. But even that was not quite the easy-going, love-all hippy product.

It was a masterpiece of imagination, put together by creative minds with no limit on time and money. *Sergeant Pepper* began, in fact, with 'Penny Lane' and 'Strawberry Fields'. Lennon and McCartney had, for a while, thought of making an album based on a consistent theme. Originally, the idea had been to centre the project around their Liverpudlian childhood. But after those two songs it ran out of steam.

Instead, the two songwriters, alone in their houses, were picking up songs from scraps read in newspapers, fragments of memory, half-recalled conversations and the atmosphere of a progressively more swinging London. The title track came first, from an idea by Paul. London was undergoing a fashion craze for resurrected military uniforms. In itself, it was ironic that a generation who had espoused the cause of peace should opt for the gaudy trappings of high patriotism and the glory of war. But everything was redefined, accepting in the bright dress uniforms a quality of peacockery, leaving behind the war-like overtones.

With this in mind, Paul began to write a song about an imaginary brass band. As a song, it didn't look as if it were destined to herald anything significant — in fact, it was one of Paul's throw-away fun pieces. Then, as The Beatles were rehearsing it, he suggested they make an album as though the Segeant Pepper band, and not The Beatles, were making the record. The Pepper bandsmen became their alter egos. It sounded fun and the others, without the impetus of touring, needed something to get their teeth into and happily complied. The whole album then took off in a remarkable way. Lennon, still dreaming his hallucinatory dreams, would have

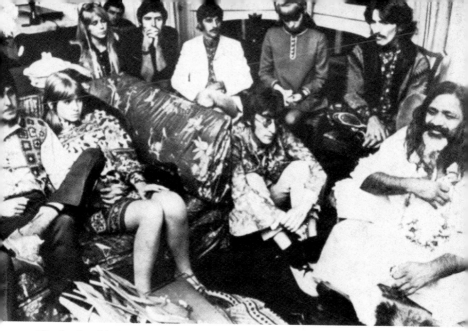

The Beatles with the Maharishi Yogi. Left-right: Paul McCartney, Jane Asher, Patti Harrison, Ringo Starr, John Lennon and George Harrison.

John Lennon and Yoko Ono hold a press conference from their bed in an Amsterdam hotel, shortly after their wedding.

Crowds in Moscow pay tribute to John Lennon.

John Lennon with his first wife Cynthia in 1964.

An early concert at a Birkenhead cinema.

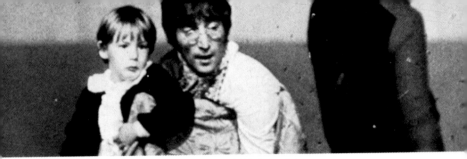

Julian Lennon with his father John.

Paul and Linda McCartney with their son James, autumn 1977.

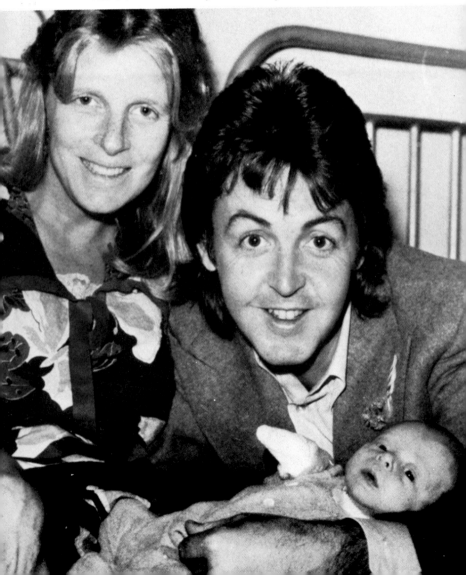

The Beatles at the time of the release of 'Sgt Pepper's Lonely Hearts Club Band'. Left-right: Paul McCartney, Ringo Starr, John Lennon, George Harrison.

John Lennon and Yoko Ono protest against the Vietnam War in 1969.

Early days. Left-right: George Harrison, Pete Best, Paul McCartney, John Lennon.

The Beatles on their first visit to Hamburg. Left-right: Paul McCartney, George Harrison, John Lennon, Ringo Starr.

The Beatles pose at a Miami press reception.

John Lennon in 1955; guitarist with The Quarry Men.

contentedly drifted off into the sunset without the outside stimulus of something to write for. Now, he was provided with a nudge and a reason to write. Neither he nor Paul went immediately into full flood, but they began to produce a steady trickle of songs.

There was John's surreal, 'Lucy In The Sky With Diamonds', Paul's short story, 'She's Leaving Home'; John's weird circus, 'Being For The Benefit Of Mr. Kite' and Paul's traffic warden lampoon, 'Lovely Rita'. *Sergeant Pepper* was wrapped up by a genuine Lennon *and* McCartney composition 'A Day In The Life', an epic song full of allusive and elusive images and powerful music.

Sergeant Pepper was liberally sprinkled with LSD. Paul had not yet admitted in public that he was taking it, and he certainly was not dropping acid in the mind-blowing quantities Lennon was. But it was there. Few, if any, of the songs are about drugs (though there are references to turning on), but the ideas and metaphors sprung from an imagination prodded by chemicals.

What drugs had done for Lennon and McCartney was to modify the way they looked at the world. Their acid experiences had not made the world seem different so much as made them look deeper inside themselves, so changing the position from which they viewed it. Drugs had not made them better adapted to reality, or even brought them closer to themselves; they just changed the focus. They were somehow more detached.

It is tempting to see *Sergeant Pepper* as a pleasant technicolour dream, where life is benign, if slightly strange. But, in the most strongly influenced Lennon songs in particular, the nightmare emerges once again. Even in 'Lucy In The Sky With Diamonds', where 'tangerine trees', 'cellophane flowers', 'newspaper taxis' and 'marmalade skies' beckon, there is a kind of claustrophobia — a feeling of being trapped in an alien world. The album's final devastating song, 'A Day In The Life', although put together in an almost random way, built up as a collage of newspaper cuttings, some of which deal with the death of a rich young acquaintance of The Beatles, is ultimately gloomy. The lyrics, as with most of Lennon and McCartney's later songs, defy analysis. There is no literal theory to hold on to. But the picture conjured up is a kind of miniature of Lennon and McCartney's life — of reading the news, absorbing the tragedy and the trivia, and escaping in a dream haze: 'Found my way upstairs and had a smoke/and somebody spoke and I went into a dream.'

Once more, there is a frightening sense of an enclosed world from which there seems only momentary, introspective escape, if not something more cataclysmic. The final section of the song is purely musical. It is, according to Lennon, 'a sound building up from nothing to the end of the world'. The forty-one piece orchestra worked from instructions passed from The Beatles via George Martin. There was no score; they played whatever came into their heads and sat in full evening dress, wearing carnival masks in an atmosphere of peculiar gaiety. The sound churns to a screeching crescendo, pauses for a heart-stopping breath, and then the final, apocalyptic echoing chord. Despite the carnival atmosphere of the recording, and the remarks by John and Paul which passed it off as just another song with drug-taking in-jokes, 'A Day In The Life' makes a strong, despairing statement. The message may be unconscious, but it's no accident.

Sergeant Pepper was released in June, 1967, to an ovation of critical rapture unrivalled even for The Beatles. The music industry, particularly the papers and the radio stations, had been waiting for months for the album to appear. The sense of expectation generated among the public was quite extraordinary. And for once, such expectations were not disappointed. The record was heralded and delivered in the nature of a royal birth, its features paraded and analysed, and its good points praised to the skies. Radio stations played the whole album from start to finish, pundits were wheeled in and out of studios, superlatives polished and put on display. As a media-event, it was hardly bettered in the whole decade.

Suddenly, pop music was *art*. It achieved respectability outside of the world of pop music and showbiz, establishing The Beatles as all-time giants and Lennon and McCartney as songwriters to be listed with the all-time greats.

Sergeant Pepper became, more than any album of the time, something that crystallised the atmosphere of the period. The heady mixture of fun, evocative poetry, mysticism and brooding clouds of insecurity summed up the feelings of a generation. The Beatles had developed from pop culture heroes into poet laureates — spokesmen and leaders.

72

It was not only the pundits who began to read deep significance into the meaning of *Sergeant Pepper*. Each individual record buyer read into this musical masterpiece their own hopes, aspirations and attitudes. It became for them a microcosmic world of fantasy, into which they allowed themselves to be drawn. Though operating on a completely different level, it worked in a similar way to J. R. R. Tolkien's masterwork *The Lord Of The Rings*. Both became the object of cult followings, both became a seminal mark of the times and the allegiances of 1960s youth.

Naturally, there was controversy too. The BBC banned 'A Day In The Life', ironically missing the real drug references but deciding the '4,000 holes in Blackburn, Lancashire' were heroin addicts' puncture marks. 'Lucy In The Sky With Diamonds', the title of a picture by Lennon's son Julian, was discovered to be a mnemonic for LSD. From then on, similar references were discovered all over the place.

But the close attention from fans and critics alike was a clear indication of the seriousness with which The Beatles were now being taken. It said less about the songs themselves than it did about the audience's need to find significance in the words of these culture heroes. There was still a search for certainty, for answers. The Beatles' followers believed that these four Liverpool geniuses would, from their elevated positions, see things more clearly than they appeared at ground level. Events were to show how wrong they were.

In the wake of *Sergeant Pepper*, Paul admitted that he had taken LSD — an announcement that caused profound shock. The Beatles had lost some of their whiter-than-white image, and Lennon was already cast as something of a bad boy following his remarks about Jesus. But Paul . . . he was the nice one. He said it had opened his eyes and given him a notion of the untapped potential of the human brain. He was roundly condemned as irresponsible. The Beatles, among others, signed a full-page advertisement in *The Times* urging marijuana law reform. Here was one of The Beatles' short-term answers to life in the 20th century.

Meanwhile, George Harrison, who had taken up the sitar to assert his personal independence within the group as much as anything else, had travelled to India to study with sitar master, Ravi Shankar. He became progressively interested in Indian

73

religion. Patti, his wife, became fascinated by a meditation technique fostered by Indian guru, Maharishi Mahesh Yogi and encouraged George to try it. He was willing, having as yet found no spiritual peace in anything to date. When the Maharishi visited London in August 1967, he also persuaded the others to sit at the guru's feet at a session at the Park Lane Hilton on August 24, 1965.

The Maharishi came into The Beatles' lives, not because they were sold on his publicity, or because he came to them. Rather, they met the Indian leader half-way. They had been looking for him, or someone like him for a while. The mind-nudging, 'tripping' drugs of 1967 had become entangled, mostly at the behest of former Harvard academic Dr Timothy Leary, with quasi-religious eastern mysticism. The notion of emptying the mind in meditation was not dissimilar to emptying the mind for LSD. Religious experiences on acid were not uncommon — even Paul had declared he had found God on acid.

But The Beatles, despite their fans' belief that they had got it all sorted out, were still looking for something else — a sense of purpose and an ability to cope. The Maharishi gave the impression of someone in touch with the essence of the universe. The Beatles, it transpired, were looking for answers as much as anyone else. 'The main thing is not to think about the future or the past. The main thing is just to get on with now', was John's version of transcendental meditation. That was what he wanted, and that was what the Maharishi was offering. A half hour's meditation per day and access to *now*.

The Beatle entourage, plus Mick Jagger and others, travelled by train to a Bangor teacher training college the next day for an immediate ten-day course under the Maharishi. Their progress was followed by the ever-present reporters and camera men alert for a new Beatle story. But any hope of immediate elevation to the sublime was smashed on Sunday morning, August 27, three days into the course. A 'phone call to The Beatles established that Brian Epstein was dead, killed by what was probably an accidental overdose of sleeping tablets. The four were shattered. Even though Epstein had for some while not been as close a presence, he was still part of their collective life.

The Beatles went to the Maharishi for wisdom. Since Brian and his death were part of the physical world, they were 'not important', he told them. Although his importance to them had diminished somewhat, his death could not be passed off so lightly. It was of grave significance. If the end of touring was the first step in a process which was, inevitably, to see the demise of The Beatles, then Epstein's death was the second.

He, more than anyone else, believed in The Beatles. For the others, the group had become a habit, albeit a productive one. But for Epstein, they were so much an extension of his life and ego that the prospect of them splitting was unthinkable. As the members took to spending more and more time as individuals, it was he, even more than Paul, who worked to keep The Beatles intact. Without him, it was Paul who would have the job of welding the unit together, even though Brian's brother Clive was taken on as acting manager.

The Beatles returned from Bangor and publicly renounced drugs, having found, as they thought, a duplicate experience in a natural form. But with *Sergeant Pepper* behind them, they lacked a project to take them forward.

Meanwhile, The Beatles signed on as fully-paid up members of the Maharishi's spiritual regeneration movement, handing over the standard disciple's once-off fee — one week's wages each. No one said how much a Beatle's working wage was computed at. In return, they were initiated into the mysteries of meditation, and hoped that peace would follow. They also undertook to spend time at the Maharishi's study centre in Rishikesh, North India.

In September, The Beatles met to consider how they might carry on without Brian. One suggestion caught their collective imaginations — or maybe it was the only one put forward. Anyway, the *Magical Mystery Tour* was born. Inevitably, the idea was Paul's. No one else seemed to have thought of anything. He had half-written a song called 'Magical Mystery Tour' for the *Sergeant Pepper* album, but it had not worked and had been left aside. In the first days of the post-Epstein Beatle era, he resurrected the song and suggested an ambitious scheme built around it.

The idea, in origin, was pure McCartney whimsey — enchanted by the memories of the English seaside resort penchant for mystery coach tours, in which holidaymakers were ferried to a picturesque destination they knew not where. Paul mused that the acid dreams and illusions of the late Sixties could make the tired, middle-aged day-trip into something extravagant and magical. His enthusiasm was infectious. They could take a bus crammed full of actors and musicians, and film the whole thing! He showed the others a diagram he had drawn, sketching the high points of the film. His ideas were still very vague but the others responded.

Without Brian, there was no one to temper their flights of imagination, no one to counsel caution or involve professional expertise. The Beatles now had sufficient confidence to feel they could tackle anything. They no longer needed the Walter Shensons and Dick Lesters who had been responsible for *A Hard Day's Night* and *Help*. This was truly a Beatles' project. They had the ideas and the money. All they needed now were the actors and camera crew. Raring to go, The Beatles even postponed their trip to India.

A coach and a camera crew were hired. So were actors — to Paul's specifications: a midget, a fat lady and extras. In September, the bus set off for the horizon via the Great West Road. From then on, everything went wrong. When they recorded, there had always been Brian Epstein to organise the cars and make sure all their requirements were met with the minimum of fuss. In the studios, there was George Martin to interpret their musical ideas and translate them into string arrangements and recording technology. Administration and technique were taken care of. But *Magical Mystery Tour* had no such administrative buffer, nor technical direction. As a consequence, the coach became snarled up in holiday traffic, and surrounded by sightseers wherever it stopped. Hotel rooms were not booked. The lack of script and overall direction for the film, which The Beatles were more or less making up as the coach and its forty-three occupants moved along, meant that shooting was chaotic.

From location, the bus was meant to move to Shepperton Studios, but as no one had booked it, a disused airfield was used. Paul directed operations there, trying to make cinematic sense of forty dwarves, a football crowd, a military band and babies in prams.

Editing began. This, too, was less than organised. No one knew who had overall control and what Paul would edit in the morning, John would re-edit in the afternoon. In the end, it was finished, and bought by BBC TV. *Magical Mystery Tour* was broadcast on Boxing Day, 1967. It was a failure. The story was a mish-mash of half thought-out ideas, indulgent, meaningless and tedious. Even the songs, 'Magical Mystery Tour', 'Fool On The Hill', 'Blue Jay Way' were extremely variable, though there were moments of quality — 'I Am The Walrus', for example. For the first time, The Beatles were panned. The tabloid papers — such great supporters of The Beatles myth — were forced to admit that this episode was a blunder. The Beatles couldn't understand it; they were shocked.

Undaunted, they rushed off into their next project. After a year and a bit, when most of the time had been spent lying fallow and thinking about what they could do, dreaming dreams of optimism and love, they were now in a hurry to *do* something. The Beatles' accountants told them they had to lose two million pounds or have it swallowed up by the Inland Revenue. They decided to open a boutique. They wanted, in Paul's words, 'A beautiful place to buy beautiful things.' The Apple Boutique in Baker Street was opened in December, 1967. It was successful in that it lost a lot of money — not least from shoplifters.

Upstairs from the boutique, The Beatles diversified further. Apple now became a publishing and record production concern; it began a retail department and an electronics division hosted by a charlatan named Magic Alex. From the start, the intention was for The Beatles to establish their own initiatives, their own administration. It was a brave attempt to remove the reins from the 'men in suits', to give total control to the young and the imaginative. It was going to be fun, it was going to be free.

But, in February, the entourage set out for India and the Maharishi's well-appointed ashram. They had promised to go earlier, but *The Magical Mystery Tour* got in the way. Here The Beatles, Mike Love of The Beach Boys, folksinger Donovan and actress Mia Farrow joined with the guru's disciples, dressing Indian-style to take up a daily schedule of fasting, meditation and chanting. Ringo couldn't face it, and arrived home saying it was 'just like Butlin's'. The others stayed. The tranquillity and the disipline agreed with them. John and Paul used the time to write songs. But, after about nine weeks, the realisation dawned independently that they were not getting anywhere. They had not found the secret of the universe. Nothing magic had happened, and the Maharishi was beginning to appear less than cosmic. Transcendental meditation was proving not to be the short cut to Nirvana the two had hoped it would be.

Rumours of the Maharishi's attempted sexual interference with Mia Farrow did nothing to ease their minds. John had a set to with the guru. He said they were going; the master asked why. John replied, 'You're the cosmic one. You ought to know.' Lennon claimed the look he received from the Maharishi was anything but loving and peaceful.

The three remaining Beatles arrived home. Even George admitted they'd made a mistake. Paul revealed that at first they had thought the Maharishi might actually be divine. But in discovering his humanity, they had been disillusioned. The episode became one more experience to leave behind.

Back in England, they threw themselves headlong into the project of the year: Apple. From Eastern meditation they moved on to an attempt at what Paul called 'western communism'. The last days of The Beatles were catching up fast.

6 We Can Work It Out

Her Majesty the Queen is reported to have said, when the Beatles first took up loving cudgels on behalf of the Maharishi, 'The Beatles are turning awfully funny, aren't they?' Her remark, to Sir Joseph Lockwood, chairman of EMI, which owned The Beatles' record company, reflected something that was passing through the minds of many of their fans. The Beatles' audience had begun a relationship with four apparently nice, uncomplicated Liverpool lads. Over the years, they had changed into complex, contradictory characters whose shifts of thinking and new directions kept their afficianados in some confusion.

This was less of a problem for those who restricted their interest to The Beatles' music — though the sound of Lennon and McCartney's songs developing and progressing was intriguing enough. But the large proportion of the young who modelled their looks and, to an extent, their ideas, on The Beatles, adapting to The Beatles' various enthusiasms, required some stamina.

In a period of nine months, the four had rushed headlong into Indian mysticism and (with the exception of George who, though turning his back on the Maharishi, still retained an Indian flavour) straight out again. Now, they were businessmen and patrons of the arts. It was gradually becoming evident that being a Beatle was not enough for them any more. The music that once held them together was now pushing them apart.

At one time, The Beatles were four parts of the same person. When asked what had happened to that sense of oneness, John said: 'They remembered that they were four individuals. You see, we believed The Beatles myth, too.' In the mid-Sixties, when The Beatles were running scared from one concert to the next, they were afraid to look outside. But, as they slowed down, as the pressure lessened, and as they began to realise there *was* a world outside, The Beatles as a phenomenon became less significant.

What Epstein's death did do was to make them look at the whole issue of the management and control of The Beatles. They realised that, despite their own personal anti-establishment feelings and their personal espousal of alternative, underground values during the late Sixties, The Beatles' business was still being run by straight businessmen.

Although by 1968 they were beginning to see that The Beatles myth *was* an illusion, they still believed sufficiently in the received wisdom that The Beatles were inviolable and multi-talented to feel that they could now take on direction and control of their own business. The had no idea how complicated it had become.

The network of companies and interests that now surrounded The Beatles was bewildering. Sorting it out and trying to win back controlling interest and revenue from their own material proved a lengthy and costly business, involving much litigation. They were forced to trust in the advice of people they were unable to check up on, and the problems tied up an enormous amount of their time and energies. The tensions that were already beginning to show between the four were exaggerated in their business dealings, so hastening the end.

But, returning from India in the spring of 1968, matters looked optimistic. Shortly before they had left for Rishikesh, what had started with the Apple Boutique had developed into record, book and electronics divisions. After they arrived back in England, they opened new premises in Wigmore Street. Along with the other divisions, it was to house 'The Apple Foundation for the Arts'. John said at the time: 'The aim of the company isn't a stack of gold teeth in the bank. We've done that bit. It's more of a trick to see if we can get the artistic freedom within the business structure, to see if we can create things and sell them without charging three times our cost.' Paul said: 'We want to help people, but without doing it for charity. *We* always had to go to the big men on our knees and touch our forelocks and say, "Please can we do so and so . . .?" We're in the happy position of not needing any more money, so, for the first time, the bosses aren't in it for profit. If you come to me and say, "I've had such and such a dream", I'll say to you, "Go away and do it".'

A full-page advertisement was put in the music papers, encouraging musicians to send their tapes to Apple. The result was predictable: the stuff came in sackfuls. Many a 'starving' artist with a bright or otherwise idea turned up on the doorstep. From its launching, the building was full of a motley collection of individuals hoping for money. Some received it, but there seemed to be no overall policy in granting bursaries. Such was the atmosphere of the times that the most potent argument for a grant was the 'vibes' given off by any specific importunate.

At the beginning, John and Paul, always the most keen and vocal in the support for the Apple idea, spent a lot of time in the place. Paul, particularly, kept almost office hours. 95 Wigmore Street had a growing staff: Apple records, film, publishing and the press office were all there. There were secretaries, cooks and office boys in abundance, few of them with much to do.

In the first flush of enthusiasm, the four Beatles would hold weekly meetings with the staff, but slowly, the directors' presence dwindled to Paul and John, and finally, just Paul. He took his responsibilities quite seriously more, it seems, because he was in love with the idea of playing offices than out of any real notion as to the outcome. He would arrive at around 9.30 a.m. to make sure the staff arrived at 10.00 and developed a passion for the minutiae of the office workings. It was he who checked regularly to make sure there was sufficient toilet paper in the ladies' loos.

Hospitality was on a lavish scale. There was plenty to drink and plenty to smoke. The kitchen supplied hot and cold meals around the clock for Beatles, staff, guests and freeloaders alike. John paid an astrologer to provide daily readings for the executives, and used the *I Ching* as a guiding rule for major policy decisions.

Apple was a busy place, of that there was no doubt, but with rare exceptions, it was fruitless. A gaggle of fans were perched perpetually on the doorstep (so regular did they become that, when the premises shifted to Savile Row, they had a proscribed hierarchy, a magazine and headed notepaper). A shifting sea of mostly charlatan artists, musicians and inventors made their way in and out of the building. The Beatles themselves played host to a stream of well-wishers from the pop aristocracy. Press officer, Derek Taylor, a personality in his own right, held court for the ever-present journalists who waited, usually in vain, for interviews with the founders. The latter found their wait made very pleasant by the rich liquid hospitality, and three or four very relaxed wordsmiths could usually be found in Taylor's domain.

By June, 1968, Wigmore Street could no longer hold all this humanity and Apple moved to 3, Savile Row — as unlikely a venue as could be imagined — surrounded by exclusive tailors of a distinguished and extremely conservative nature. Money continued to pour out of the organisation. The two million pound taxable surplus was well on the way to being spent.

Two Apple initiatives met with some success. Apple records, under the guiding hand of Peter Asher (Jane's brother, formerly of the duo, Peter and Gordon), managed to build a roster of talent: Badfinger, Jackie Lomax, James Taylor and Mary Hopkins, among others. It was not wildly adventurous but there was some success. Surprisingly, the highlight of the year was not an Apple creation but a project originally initiated by Brian Epstein. It was a cartoon film based on Beatles songs and written by *Love Story* author, Erich Segal: *Yellow Submarine*. The Beatles used some old songs and wrote new ones for the movie. Although, for the first time, their energies and interest were not galvanised and the subsequent album was patchy and weak, the film was a resounding success with the public. Erich Segal's witty script and the flair and originality of the visuals were such that The Beatles were relegated to an almost incidental role.

Meanwhile, back in Baker Street, the Apple boutique was proving problematic. Its initiators, Dutch hippy designers, had spent little time looking after the shop but had rather borrowed, on long-term, over a period of time, the best items of stock. The arty, dim interior had proved a boon for shoplifters and some of the staff were fiddling the tills. On July 31, 1968, it was closed down. The Beatles' wives and girlfriends had first pick of the garments and the rest were given away in a gadarene scramble. The public took everything they could lay their hands on, including shop-fittings. It was not the dignified face of a free society The Beatles would have wanted.

The Apple enterprise was foundering. The berobed children of peace were proving as unscrupulous as the men in suits. It was all rather bewildering. The Apple offices were still chaotic and unproductive. Apple press produced no books (there was a room full of untouched manuscripts); the film division produced no films (*Yellow Submarine* was done by United Artists); the Apple Foundation for the Arts was a farce. Lennon admitted: 'Apple was a manifestation of Beatle naivety, collective naivety. We said, "We're going to do this and help everybody", and all that and we got conned on the subtlest and bluntest level. We really didn't get approached by the best artists; we got all the bums from everywhere else, all the ones that everyone had thrown out. The ones who were really groovy wouldn't approach us because they were too proud. We had to quickly build up another wall round us to protect us from all the beggars and lepers in Britain and America who came to see us. Our lives were getting insane! I tried, when we were in Wigmore Street, to see everyone, day in and day out, and there wasn't anyone who had anything to offer to society or me or anything. There was just, "I want, I want and why not?"'

He sounded surprised. Collective naivety was an understatement. The alternative culture of the late 1960s was smitten by a fantasy view of human nature which managed neatly to sidestep the evidence of the past. 'If only we, the children of Aquarius, could be in charge, we could open things up', was the thought behind the movement. The creation of an ideal society was only a matter of will and resources, they imagined. The Beatles had bought the package. Even John, the cynic, the deflator of pretension seemed somehow to have hit a temporary blind spot. Paul, too, always the most cautious, managed to throw instinctive judgement to the wind in the belief that their benevolence would be accepted in the spirit in which it was given.

Drugs, the conventional wisdom of the age, and wishful thinking each had a hand in the building and demolition of Apple. John's enormous appetite for drugs and the sensation they supplied, and even Paul's more tentative explorations in the area, led them to imagine much that was not real or possible. Tripping, or just gently stoned, it was easy to think that people could change, that greed could be overturned by altruism. The cliché of the Aquarian age was that if individuals could get their heads together, with everyone doing their own thing in mutual tolerance and love, the world would be transformed. You only had to try.

The problem was that The Beatles fell in love with paradise and thought that it could be achieved by doling out money. There was an element of conscience-salving too, as The Beatles realised that their riches ought to be channelled profitably for the cause of society. In that respect, they were genuine. But they had neither the stamina, the strategy nor the understanding to come to terms with the dirty work of dealing with people. They had lived in an unreal world for too long.

As Apple was launched and grew, John Lennon was undergoing further change. He had not yet fallen in love, but, while he was in Rishikesh, he had written long and often to Yoko Ono. He was most definitely impressed by her. In the dark days before the Maharishi, when he sat for long hours, staring into space, his meditation was occasionally disturbed by enigmatic postcards from Yoko saying, 'Watch the light until dawn'. She fascinated him.

Over the years, The Beatles had become a job of work. He was still writing closely with Paul, but not quite as close as before and, though the songs were sometimes brilliant, life had little spark for Lennon. Suddenly, this woman had appeared on the scene, talking of a different world, in a different language. He said: 'As she was talking to me, I'd be getting higher and higher. Then she'd leave and I'd go back to this sort of suburbia. Then I'd meet her again and my head would open, like I was on an acid trip.'

Back in Weybridge, after the Indian trip, changes developed in John's and Cynthia's relationship. Cynthia had always accepted the role of the stay-at-home wife that John had carved out for her. John's less-than-monastic activities on tour as a Beatle had been kept from her. Cyn knew that she was only John's wife because she had become pregnant, and that John's interests and his mind were a long way from hers. But she still had some hope for their marriage. There was certainly no animosity.

At first, Yoko seemed not to be a threat — more of a joke. But progressively, she seemed to be creeping between them. John had admitted only recently that he had not been entirely faithful to Cynthia, even though, at this stage, nothing had happened between him and Yoko. He constantly denied there was anyone else.

But all the time, Yoko and her world seemed more and more

alluring. John had reacted to the art scene with some suspicion at first, and ever after he remained only on its fringes. He despised intellectuals and he hated the pretentiousness and high seriousness of the avant garde scene. But Yoko seemed both to love it and, at the same time, to poke fun at it. Lennon could respond to that.

For him, it was a fresh area. Having dabbled in the art world as a student, he now saw in it a potential for freedom and wild experimentation hitherto closed to him. At art school, he had been expected to follow fairly rigid patterns of learning. In The Beatles, the commercial aspects had restricted his output and approach within definite limits. But in the avant garde, anything went. The avant garde existed in order to create new modes of expression, to break down artistic barriers. Communications and commercial viability were not issues that counted.

Yoko took him by the hand, led him into a life of new dimensions. Their relationship moved on to a different footing. John brought Yoko over while Cynthia was away. He took her up to his studio, played her his most weird tapes, including some electronic music. 'She was suddenly impressed,' said Lennon, 'then she said, "Let's make one ourselves". So we made *Two Virgins* (the title of the first Lennon/Ono album collaboration). It was midnight when we started *Two Virgins*; it was dawn when we finished and then we made love at dawn. It was very beautiful.'

Those were not the sentiments of Cynthia when she arrived home to find John and Yoko together. The six-year marriage was over. 'My marriage to Cyn was not unhappy', said Lennon, 'but it was just a normal marital state where nothing happened and which we continued to sustain. You sustain it until you meet someone who really sets you alight. With Yoko, I really knew love for the first time.'

The physical and intellectual partnership grew from there. From that point on, the two were inseparable. From that point on, John's relationship with The Beatles changed. In fact, the Yoko Ono/John Lennon axis was of such importance that The Beatles were never the same again.

Lennon, in early 1968, had been tortured as to what he should make of the student riots spreading all over Europe. The Daniel Cohn-Bendits and the Tariq Alis were throwing revolutionary rhetoric all over the place. It was then that he had first written a song to be released later in the year called simply, 'Revolution'. He was going through one of his periodic bouts of depression at the time, and was torn between his desire to radicalise the world and his desire to retreat back into himself. Consequently, he had written two versions of the song — one in which he identified with the struggle and the other in which he detached himself. In the end, he plumped for the second in which, he said, 'You can count me out.' With that matter temporarily decided and the Maharishi out of the way, his alliance with Yoko helped provide the certainty in his life that he had long been looking for. He leant heavily on her. In August, Cynthia sued John for divorce, citing Yoko Ono.

Paul's love-life was, if no less complicated, a little less fraught. His relationship with Jane Asher had continued. The combination was a good one, each independent, yet respecting the other's role and professional involvement. There had been much talk in the press about their possible engagement and at Christmas, 1967, they announced that they were to be married, although the date was unspecified. It was no secret that Paul had had casual affairs during the time he and Jane were together, though she apparently knew nothing of them, until she stumbled on one, causing an understandable rift.

But the relationship stabilised and, with their mutual love and affection so consistent and, it seemed, so deep, things looked set fair. Even Jane's return from a theatre tour in 1967 to find Paul immersed in LSD did nothing to shake them up, even though she refused adamantly to have anything to do with acid. But, in July, it was announced that wedding plans were off. No explanation was given.

A few lightning affairs later, Paul met Linda Eastman — an American girl from a rich, East Coast family, who had turned against the mores of her parents, taken up photography in a semi-professional way and was given to hanging around rock stars. Paul met her in a London club, the Bag o' Nails. She was completely different from Jane Asher. Much less cool and independent than Jane, she was essentially a rock generation person. It was her life, her chief aim to be around rock music and rock musicians. She was a fan, too. Whereas Jane Asher treated Paul as an equal and had given only as much to him as he to her, Linda immediately took the more subservient, more supportive role. Linda Eastman was good for McCartney's ego

— she devoted herself to him. She helped him believe in himself, making him more decisive and confident in his own abilities.

Because she devoted herself to him, she changed Paul more than Jane had. Under her influence, he became more relaxed, scruffier, tubbier and down-home for a while. He began to look less to John for standards in songwriting. Linda also had a little girl, Heather, from her first marriage. From the start Paul acted the father. He loved it.

One of Paul's best songs dates from the time of the break-up with Jane and his search for a new partner. It was The Beatles' summer single, their eighteenth and, interestingly, it formed a double 'A'-side with John's 'Revolution'. The song, 'Hey Jude', was emotional, but for once it avoided sentimentality. It was written to himself, urging him to be more committed this time: 'You're waiting for someone to perform with', it ran, 'remember to let her under your skin/then you'll begin to make it better.' Even John was taken by it and thought for a while it was an encouragement to him in his relationship with Yoko.

But Paul had no such encouragement in mind. His sympathies were with Cynthia. In fact, he made a visit to comfort her when John took up with Yoko. Lennon's three partners took an instant dislike to Yoko. She was not part of their conception of Beatle women. It was not so much that she was bright, or that she had a career of her own, but that she wanted to be involved in every part of John's life at an equal level. John accepted this quite readily. He was very much in love with Yoko and was pleased to share in her initiatives and to make her part of his. They had become an artistic partnership and had already put on at least one gallery show together.

The other three Beatles had first met Yoko when she came with John to an Abbey Road recording session in early spring. But she did not stay behind the control room glass, she came into the recording arena and sat with John. The intimacy of the couple was remarkable. John had never been like this before. But the others decided not to take the relationship seriously. They referred to Yoko as 'the flavour of the month' — yet another of John's phases.

However, when recording began in May, 1968, for The Beatles' next album, Yoko was still there. She arrived with John on the first day of recording. Just as before, she ignored the seats of the control room and sat in with John throughout. Yoko's physical presence in the studio was a constant irritant to the others. They had always jealously guarded the idea of the foursome as being a unity. Earlier suggestions that George Martin, because of his contribution to *Sergeant Pepper,* was the fifth Beatle had been firmly squashed by both John and Paul. The Beatles had shut Brian Epstein out when he made attempts to involve himself in the music, so they were not about to tolerate Yoko Ono.

In truth, she never made suggestions as to how The Beatles should record. But the others — George and Paul in particular — saw her as having a strong influence on John. Paul, especially, had little sympathy with John's essays into the world of the avant garde, and he disliked Lennon's increasing tendency to preach publicly about the ills of society. He felt that since Yoko had come on the scene, John's music had become more harsh and strident.

John's partnership with Yoko had led him to a more uncompromising position regarding his music. He began to see himself more as a fine artist whose musical statements were inviolate. This made him more difficult to deal with in the studio where previously there had been a genuine spirit of give and take. It also made him less tolerant of Paul's easy melodies and tendency to be facile and sentimental.

So, when The Beatles plus Yoko met to start recording what was to become *The Beatles* or the *White Album,* as it was popularly known, there was a sense of strain. It could have been a great record. Both John and Paul had a large backlog of songs, many of them written in India — thirty between them. George had begun to mature as a songwriter and had some of his best material ever to contribute. Even Ringo had brought a song with him.

But it was not to be. The songs each individual brought remained as pretty well final songs. When they played them to each other, the usual suggestions and modifications were not forthcoming. No one could raise the energy and enthusiasm to like the other's songs enough. The vital spark of collaboration that had kept The Beatles' music sane, stopped either Lennon or McCartney from going over the edge, the infusion of fresh ideas for a middle-eight or a change of line was absent. It was tragic.

Early on, it had been decided that, with the wealth of material available, they would make a double album, to be sold as one package. It had never been done before outside the classical music field. But it *could* have worked had The Beatles been able to blend as a unit. John said, 'We made the double album, the set. It's like if you took each track off it and made it all mine and all George's . . . it was just me and a backing group, Paul and a backing group . . . We broke up then.'

Without the necessary spark to lift many of the songs out of the ordinary, it soon became obvious to all but The Beatles that there were not really enough good songs for a double album. George Martin tried to suggest that they cut down and make a single excellent album. The Beatles refused even to think of the idea. In that one, small thing, they were unanimous. Over the rest, there were arguments and bad feeling. Paul felt John's electronic version of what could happen if revolution did take place — the anarchic 'Revolution Number Nine' — was over the top and should be cut. John thought 'Ob-la-di, Ob-la-da' was trite.

Ringo couldn't stand the bickering. He, after all, had less to do than the rest once the rhythm tracks were laid down. Halfway through the five months it took to record, he announced that he was playing badly, had had enough and was resigning. A week later, he was back. There were flowers and welcome messages on his drum kit from George.

But John and Paul were individually talented enough, despite their excesses, to produce some fireworks and there *are* some classic songs on the album. George Martin was right: there was about one album's worth. George took advantage of the gap in the usually united front of Paul and John to get in more songs than usual.

Paul had a good rocker in 'Back In The USSR', a beautiful ballad in 'Blackbird', plus a number of little ditties. John's product was biting and often indulgent, but he had his moments too, notably on the screaming 'Helter Skelter' (the song that mass killer Charles Manson claimed was his instruction to kill Sharon Tate). He took the opportunity, in hindsight, to give tribute to what he considered to be the two main women in his life. In a gentle song entitled, 'Julia', he blended the personalities of his mother and Yoko into one and sang of his love to both.

Nevertheless, all these are fragments. The album was a collection of bits and pieces and, although when it was released in November, 1968, it received esctatic reviews, it stands as a memorial to the death of The Beatles. John Lennon and Paul

McCartney needed each other. It has become a truism now, but The Beatles myth was so strong in 1968 that no one saw past it into the story the music was telling.

The Beatles' music was still a strong factor in the lives of their millions-strong audience. The *White Album,* as all before it, was subjected to the minutest analysis by pundits and fans alike. Even John's sly poke at the analysts in one of the album's songs, 'Glass Onion' (where he referred to a number of past Beatle songs) made no difference. The Beatles were still seen as spokesmen. Already, in 1968, the hippy culture was breaking up and there was a determined move towards militancy in student groups. John's statements in 'Revolution' came as a grave disappointment to them. But the foursome's implicit stance as counter-culture figures still made them heroes.

By now, music was seen as the universal language which united youth. The serious US rock paper, *Rolling Stone,* was calling it 'the Rock Culture', and The Beatles the king figures. The Beatles' unity was of extreme importance to them. Their very presence was an active voice (albeit, a none too coherent one). They had, after all, beaten the system. They had risen to the top, had used the record industry to put across values that stood against those of the record company magnates. And, of course, they had started Apple. They were ploughing back their millions into the cause.

They were. But progressively, it showed itself as little more than a futile gesture. Apple was rotting gently. The organisation continued to be ripped off, and those controlling the purse strings were at their wits end as to how to stop it. The Beatles, just as Lennon said, built additional barriers to protect themselves from the madness. They had started by trying to open things out and attempting to take an active part in the running of their company, but they ended up just as they had on tour, before it all started, locked away in their own domain. They treated 3 Savile Row like a club. Driving in, calling down to the kitchen for food, and getting on with business.

Following their initiation into the world of transcendental meditation, The Beatles had announced that they had given up drugs, but it was only a temporary measure. They soon returned, though not quite to the same degree. Marijuana was certainly a part of The Beatles' daily Apple routine. They kept stashes at home, too. So far, the police, for reasons best known to themselves, didn't bother them.

But, on October 18, when John and Yoko were in bed in the flat they had borrowed from Ringo, the police raided. They found an ounce-and-a-half of cannabis. John and Yoko were arrested and taken to Marylebone Police Station. The forces of law and order, it seemed, were no longer willing to believe in The Beatles myth. John pleaded guilty, cleared Yoko of any blame and received a fine of £150 plus £20 costs — a small fine for a Beatle. But his conviction was to create a great deal more trouble when, in the Seventies, he was refused immigration papers for the USA.

The hearing took place in November, a mixed month for The Beatles. John and Yoko took full-page advertisements launching an appeal for 'The Peace Ship', an independent, neutral radio station broadcasting to both sides in the Middle East. Cynthia Lennon was granted a decree nisi. The electronic album, *Two Virgins,* recorded by John and Yoko, was released. It sported a cover featuring the happy couple in full frontal nudity. EMI refused to distribute it but another company was found and copies were sold in brown paper bags. Yoko said of the cover, 'It's art.' John said, 'If people practised being themselves instead of pretending what they aren't, there would be peace.'

The *White Album* was also released, while John was with Yoko in hospital. She had been expecting a baby by Lennon, but a miscarriage was threatened and she lost the baby the day the album came out. John lay in the bed next to Yoko's in her room in Queen Charlotte's hospital. He refused to leave her.

Yoko recovered, and the pair made an appearance at a thinly-attended Christmas extravaganza at the Royal Albert Hall. Called the *Alchemical Wedding,* it was a showcase of the new underground arts. John and Yoko appeared inside a large bag which rolled about on stage in front of the largely mystified audience.

Over the Christmas time, Paul worked hard on his partners to return to live performances. Their singles that year — 'Lady Madonna', 'Hey Jude', 'Revolution' — were all eminently playable, being far less complex than the *Sergeant Pepper* material. The same was true of many of the songs on the *White*

Album. Paul badly missed the audience but the others were not convinced. Still, they compromised, deciding to film the sessions for their next album. It was their intention to do the album straight, to all intents and purposes, live.

Rehearsals began on January, 2, 1969, on the sound stage of Twickenham Film Studios. Paul as initiator of the idea felt bound to make it a success. But, even with his energies, playing in daylight, in a freezing barn-like building was not easy to enjoy. Paul was at his schoolmasterly worst, pushing George particularly to the end of his tether. There was little response to his despairing enthusiasm. This time, George upped and left, tired of being got at by Paul. But he returned, too.

They had planned to record in the 72-track studio the mysterious Magic Alex was meant to be building at the Apple offices. But Magic Alex, head of Apple Electronics, who had talked The Beatles out of many thousands for his hare-brained schemes, none of which seemed to surface, had not even put a console in the skeleton studio. The only way George Martin could get suitable facilities was to ship in rented equipment.

Over a hundred songs, old and new, were recorded. They did enormous numbers of takes, the first one sounding just like the last, and all on film. At length, The Beatles gave a final (and, as it turned out, farewell) live performance on the roof of the Apple buildings. They then left all the material in the can for someone else to deal with. It went to Phil Spector, whose hits in the early Sixties by The Ronettes and The Crystals had made him one of the myth figures of pop. Who else could be given the chance to produce a Beatles' album? It was to take him a long time to sort it all out.

Meanwhile, Apple was in such a mess, that even The Beatles realised it would have to be sorted out. Their personal reserves were running low, and Apple was losing a reported £20,000 a week. They began looking for a big man to control it, and even approached Lord Beeching, the axeman of British Rail. Lennon announced, 'If it carries on like this, we'll be broke in six months.'

Mick Jagger recommended The Rolling Stones' manager, Allen Klein, one of the sharper operators in the already knife-edged world of the music business. Paul didn't like him. He suggested Linda's father, Lee Eastman, a New York lawyer. Things got more complicated. Lord Beeching told John that

The Beatles would do better to stick to making records. But by now they had become so involved in the workings of the Apple empire that, for the next year, a larger proportion of their time was spent in business meetings. No longer could they depute to an Epstein figure the task of 'looking after the percentages'.

Protracted and tangled legal hassles ensued, surrounding the selling and buying of Beatles' holdings and companies. A personal animosity grew between Eastman and Klein (who became officially The Beatles' manager — though Paul never accepted it). Their battle reflected the growing estrangement and eventual hostilities between Paul and John.

In between times, there was other activity. Paul married Linda Eastman on March 12. The same night, while George was away, the drugs squad raided his home and recovered 570 grains of cannabis. On March 20, John and Yoko, on holiday in Paris, made a half-day trip to Gibraltar where they were married.

1969 was, for John and Yoko, a Peace year. Their honeymoon took the form of a bed-in for peace in the Amsterdam Hilton. Floods of reporters and photographers flocked to their bedside expecting nothing less from the crazy Beatle than a sex-show, or at least some dramatic copy. Instead, they got John and Yoko in pyjamas and some peaceful propaganda.

Later for the Austrian TV début of a John and Yoko film called *Rape* (in which an unsuspecting girl was harried by a camera crew until she broke down), the couple appeared, once more, in a bag. 'Bagism' did not prejudice the listener by a distracting personal appearance, said John. More bagism would mean more peace. May 30 saw the release of 'The Ballad Of John And Yoko', the last ever Beatle single that could be properly described as a Lennon and McCartney collaboration. It was John's song throughout, about his struggle for peace and his paranoia at what he considered establishment persecution. Paul was nice enough to help him out on bass and drums.

By this time, John and Yoko had held a second bed-in for peace in the Montreal Hilton. For the next two months, he and Yoko contrived to dominate the media for peace by virtue of their personal news value.

It would be nice to think that it worked. But such was the press and such was Lennon's curious ability to make his public statements seem part of a transition, he became, to British eyes at least, just one more eccentric millionaire with a bee in his bonnet.

May had also witnessed the release of John and Yoko's second electronic noises album, *Life With The Lions* — much to the embarrassment of the other three partners. In the meantime, Alan Klein had been sacking vast numbers of Apple staff, even Ron Kass and Peter Asher, between them responsible for selling sixteen million copies of Apple records.

But, late in July, a curious event happened. Amid all the estrangement and animosity, The Beatles somehow managed to agree to record once more. Paul 'phoned George Martin and said they wanted to record an album 'the way we used to'. Martin agreed, on condition that all The Beatles would be like they used to be. They were. Quite how it happened is not clear. But, in July and August, everyone put aside their quarrels, their own burgeoning solo activities, to be The Beatles again. Perhaps the pressure was off and, knowing that The Beatles were finished, they could act it all out for fun. Or perhaps it was a desperate attempt at a second honeymoon to save the marriage. Whatever it was, they did come together.

The result was *Abbey Road*. Although *Let It Be*, the album of the film, was chronologically the last Beatles album, *Abbey Road* was, in real terms, their swan song. A marvellous opus, it showed just how far they had come, though nothing any of them has done since compares. The mutual challenge brought together some of the finest songs of Paul, John and George. Musically, it contained some of the best playing ever by all four of them. George's guitar lines have a fluidity he must have learned from his great friend, Eric Clapton. Ringo's drumming was simple, but eloquent. And John and Paul let their instruments speak as well as they ever did. *Abbey Road* shared the inner unity, the sense of singleness of purpose that *Sergeant Pepper* had. Each track flowed into the next.

When it came out on September 26, 1969, it revived hopes in The Beatles camp that all was well again, even though John and Yoko had also released a single called 'Give Peace A Chance' under the name of The Plastic Ono Band — a non-existent unit.

As the album came out, on a whim, John accepted an invitation to play a rock'n'roll revival concert in Toronto, next day. He and Yoko put together a real Plastic Ono Band, featuring Eric Clapton and Klaus Voormann.

When he returned, Paul tried to persuade him to go on tour with The Beatles. In the wake of *Abbey Road*, George and Ringo were amenable. But John, having tested the waters of live performance himself, wanted to do it on his own terms. 'I'm leaving the group,' he said. 'I've had enough. I want a divorce.' But even John's resignation did not take effect. Allen Klein persuaded him he should stay until delicate contract negotiations were finished. Even so, bitter arguments broke out between John and Paul. John told him he hated Paul's 'granny music', and that he felt he had always had to fight for space on albums.

The only question now was, *who* was actually going to leave? Tired of the recriminations and Klein's constant business wrangles, Paul retreated with Linda, Heather and newly-born daughter Mary to his Argyllshire farm. His sudden disappearance coincided with a rumour which shoved all future Beatles speculations aside: Paul was dead, said an anonymous 'phone caller to a Detroit Radio station. Evidence could be seen on the *Abbey Road* sleeve. It was typical American Beatle-fan lunacy, unquenchable even by Paul's re-appearance. A 'Paul is dead' industry grew up. Magazines, articles and even rock singles worked on the possibilities. The innocent photograph of the Beatles walking across the zebra crossing in Abbey Road was searched for clues — Paul had no shoes on, he was walking out of step. Other 'evidence' was dug up. It was real silly season stuff, but it sold a lot of Beatles records.

John brought out another single in October, 'Cold Turkey', a celebration of pain. He had taken to heroin 'because of what The Beatles and others were doing to us. But we got out of it.' John had wanted it to be the next Beatle single, but the others had turned it down. In November, Lennon sent back his MBE, 'in protest against Britain's involvement in the Nigeria-Biafra thing, against our support of America in Vietnam, and against "Cold Turkey" slipping down the charts!'

Paul had been recording his own album on which he played almost all the instruments and sang his own songs. There was no editing or production from anyone else. It was unexpurgated Paul. He asked Apple for an April 10 release. The other Beatles and Klein said no. An April 1970 release for Paul would clash with the release of *Let It Be*, which Spector had managed to salvage. Paul persisted, and *Let It Be* was put back. His very mixed and unsatisfactory solo album was released to mixed and unsatisfied reviews. Paul alone was not a winner, it seemed. A self-interview was included on the album sleeve. He cited 'personal differences, business differences, musical differences' as reason for not continuing The Beatles. Sneaky Paul had stolen the march on everyone else.

The cards were on the table. The Beatles were no more. On May 20, *Let It Be* came out — the last Beatle album. It was a patchy, scissors-and-paste job by Spector and it showed. Both the film and the record served as a postscript to The Beatles. Sadly, there was no trumpet, no cataclysmic end, but frienaships rarely end that way. Already, legal proceedings were being undertaken to disentangle the four from each other. It came out as a sad commentary on what can happen when great talents lose their direction. They became four wasted talents.

The end was a long time coming and, even when it arrived, no one could accept it. Right up to John Lennon's death, Beatle reunion hopes and rumours would be regularly trotted out. But it was never on. The Beatles were finished.

Why did The Beatles break-up? Why did Lennon and McCartney part? The questions have often been asked and will be asked again. There is no one word answer and it is not difficult to see why. Some people believe they were finished as soon as they stopped playing to live audiences. Others lay all the blame at Yoko's door. The death of Brian Epstein has been seen as the real sign of the end, while Allen Klein's appearance on the scene has been pointed to as the factor which set The Beatles at each other's throats.

In truth, it was all these things. But the break-up of The Beatles is really rooted in the break-up of Lennon and McCartney. When they were touring, they hardly had any separate lives outside The Beatles. John and Paul were under constant pressure to keep producing. They didn't trust the others to create material of sufficient quality and their own differences in temperament, character and musical bent fired their joint creativity. They enjoyed their differences. Each was excited by the music the other was producing *because* it was so different from his own.

When they stopped touring, they were forced to keep their own company and counsel. They began to develop again as individuals, to pick up the reins of their own lives once more. Alone, their differences in taste, attitude, lifestyle and personality became emphasised. But they weren't finished yet; they still needed The Beatles. They had to keep getting together to reinforce their sense of identity. They were not yet ready to go it alone. As *Sergeant Pepper* showed, they were still sparking off each other's ideas.

When Brian died, there is no doubt that it was one more step toward The Beatles' demise. He was the one person close to them, yet outside, who had really made it his life's work to keep The Beatles alive. He existed almost solely for them, and through them. The partnership might have crumbled then, but Paul, believing there was some purpose in the group, kept things moving. He bullied and chivvied them into subsequent projects.

The birth of Apple — essentially a joint project — kept them together, but, by this stage, the writing partnership was breaking up. John, in particular, was beginning to see The Beatles as a job. His interests were diversifying madly, and his love for the Lunatic fringe of experimentation was taking him away. But, until spring 1968, The Beatles were still the main focus in his life. He could not stand on his own.

Then he fell in love with Yoko Ono. While it is not a matter of blaming Yoko for the break-up of the band and the Lennon/McCartney team, John's partnership with Yoko was the final cause for the split. She brought to Lennon's life a whole new range of experiences — a new way of looking at the world. He found in her an ally, someone who sympathised with his fascination with the absurd and the fringe world of the avant garde. She came from that world herself, and encouraged it.

With such a partner, John could try out all the odd musical and artistic fancies he had ever had — the ones Paul persuaded him were not part of The Beatles' ethos. In short, he found that he did not need The Beatles any more. Yoko made him a complete person more than Paul did. In fact, she never complemented him the way McCartney managed to. Paul was the reverse side of Lennon's coin. That was what made them such a dynamic partnership. Yoko was very similar to John. What they encouraged in each other was excess and adventure.

The other Beatles, and Paul in particular, felt, rightly, that they had lost John to Yoko. She came between them and they could never forgive her that. The ensuing estrangement

97

between Lennon and McCartney meant they could never work together again. Simply, they were not the same people. Paul failed to understand John's new artiness and propensity to preach, while John began to despise Paul's easy melodies and sentiment.

The Beatles hung on a thread for a while, throughout the recording of the *White Album, Let It Be* and *Abbey Road,* largely because of Paul's energies. He still believed in The Beatles. But then, Paul's outside relationships changed. He left the cool, detached Jane Asher — his equal. He met Linda Eastman. She was a fan. She doted on him, reassured him in John's absence that he was a good writer and a great performer. She made him believe in himself. She brought a child to their marriage, and seven months later another child was born. Parenthood gave a new dimension to Paul's life. He realised, in a way John never had, the inestimable values and qualities of the family. He loved it and took inordinate pride in his children.

Paul, too, had found a substitute for The Beatles and, most important, a substitute for John. Just as Yoko brought out the extremes in John's character, so the family did in Paul. His love for his wife and kids spilled over into saccharin emotion.

With the two thus divided, neither needing The Beatles to prop up their egos or as a vehicle for their songs (they knew they were individually popular enough to make it alone), how could The Beatles survive? The answer is history. Despite all attempts from within and without to reunite them, The Beatles were finished. All hopes were finally dashed by John Lennon's tragic death on December 8, 1980.

7 Paul: Don't Let It Bring You Down

Paul was on his own. The release of his do-it-yourself album, *McCartney*, pre-empted the end of The Beatles, and his announcement that he had left the group brought the proceedings to a standstill. In December, 1970, McCartney started High Court proceedings to end The Beatles' partnership and, on March 10, a Receiver was appointed to wind up the affairs.

In January of that year, Paul bought an extra four hundred acres of land adjacent to his farm, High Park, near Campbelltown, Argyllshire on the Mull of Kintyre. It was a significant move: he was extending his home base — the centre from which he would operate from then on. He retained Linda's father, Lee Eastman, as his attorney and set up a small office in London to conduct his affairs.

Lee Eastman had given some advice to Paul. It was the kind of avuncular wisdom his dad might have dished out: 'Make sure you stay ordinary'. For a genuine superstar and millionaire whose reputation was built by teenage adulation, McCartney has kept to his father-in-law's advice. He has remained, when it suits him, open and friendly with the press and accessible to his public. Those who have met him have remarked on his facility to make each person he talks with feel they are the only one in the room. It is part of his nature.

McCartney is not perfect. He came out badly from the court proceedings that brought a legal end to The Beatles, partly because he submitted most of his evidence in writing, making him appear distant and carping. Always, he was the one to be sneaky, rather than transparent, when it came to difficult personal relationships.

But the charm, the keenness, is not part of an elaborate front. It *is* a kind of façade, but it is as much a part of him as the real Paul which lurks behind it. It is this real Paul that no-one, except his closest friends and family, know. He has a deep detachment which is protected by his affable exterior. It comes out most, perhaps, in his poetic songs, in his insecurity about newly written numbers which he has to play over to friends for approval, and in his deep-rooted need to perform, to be out there in front of people.

His career since leaving The Beatles has been an unqualified commercial success. He always came across as the nicest of the four, and this stood him in good stead for his solo career. He would never be the one to appeal to the hard core rock fans or to the more serious minded for whom John was the man to follow. Instead, he was able to capitalise on the broad, middle range pop market that The Beatles captured. For them, he has remained the baby-faced Beatle with the beautiful voice and the catchy melody.

But his solo flight did not take off smoothly. The *McCartney* album, on which Paul played all the instruments, was a kind of 'I can do my own thing, too' response to John's multiplying extra-curricular activities as a Beatle. It was almost universally panned by the music press, an indulgent, primitive album whose charm existed only for McCartney camp followers.

Subsequently, he worked in mirror image to Lennon. Whereas Yoko initiated John into a new world of fine art freedom, so that John and Yoko became a team, Paul brought Linda, who had no real musical background, into the rock world as a performer. He taught her to play piano and urged her to take a full part in his professional as well as private life. Probably he did so less out of a concern to show that he could beat John in the marriage partnership stakes than for the genuine need actively to share his music with someone.

For Paul, The Beatles had been his life. He needed the group; it was imperative to be involved with other people — to bounce ideas off them. In the fallow period before he formed his own band, Linda played an essential musical role. By his second album, *Ram*, the two had become one: it was credited to Paul and Linda McCartney. They even began writing together, although Linda entirely lacked the steel provided by Lennon.

From the start, McCartney songs were marked by a lightness of touch and deceptive easiness of style became characteristic. But, with very rare exceptions, the truism is all too plainly accurate. Without John, the songs lack bite. They are benign and flabby, but almost flawlessly put together, very catchy and highly successful. McCartney knows his trade. As a solo songwriter he will rank with the greats — not the rock poet greats such as Bob Dylan, Paul Simon, even Jackson Browne or Joni Mitchell — but the showbiz/pop greats like Neil Sedaka, Neil Diamond or the very best of the Tamla Motown stable.

It was all very well, Paul and his wife writing songs up on the Mull of Kintyre, but McCartney needed a vehicle for his music. That meant a group. He was content for a while to play with the kids, drive the tractor about in mud-encrusted wellington boots and grow his vegetables. But it wasn't long before he began to hanker for that moment when he could step on stage under the lights and work his wiles on an audience. Before The Beatles had broken up, he had been within an inch of persuading them to make a few appearances — even in disguise. So, it was inevitable that Paul should begin to look around for musicians to join him.

It was typical of his thoroughness that when he auditioned for a drummer, he should have a really beat-up drum-kit for his nine interviewees to use. He figured that anyone good enough to cope on that poor equipment would be great on the best. That was how Dannie Seiwell came to be recruited. Later, he was joined by Denny Lane, formerly of The Moody Blues. Lane was to become McCartney's big buddy and the one other constant member of the band, apart from Linda, throughout numerous personnel changes. Henry McCullough on lead guitar was added and rehearsals began. They became Paul McCartney and Wings.

Their first album, *Wings Wild Life*, was released in December, 1971. Their first single, an unprecedented political essay by McCartney, 'Give Ireland Back To The Irish', was banned by the BBC and failed to reach the top of the charts. Perhaps Paul was still dogging John's footsteps. The single was released in January, 1972, only a month after John and Yoko's 'Happy Christmas/War Is Over'.

These early days of McCartney's new career were bedevilled by verbal attacks from John, who was both complaining about

Paul's attitude over the court proceedings to wind up The Beatles (he claimed his delays had cost them one million pounds), and about his music. On his October, 1971 album, *Imagine,* Lennon ripped into Paul with a song called 'How Do You Sleep', in which he described Paul's efforts as 'muzak to my ears'. It was a tiny bit tit-for-tat, since Paul had made cutting remarks about too much 'preaching' in one of his songs.

But Paul, althought he usually forbore to reply to Lennon's attacks which came via the press, was inevitably affected by the slurs. 'I sat down and pored over every little paragraph. "Does he really think that of me," I thought. And, at the time, I thought, "It's me. I am. That's just what I'm like. He's captured me so well; I'm a turd, you know." I sat and thought, "I'm just nothing." But then people who dug me, like Linda, said, "You know that's not true, you're joking. He's got a grudge man; the guy's trying to polish you off." Gradually, I started to think, "Great, that's not true. I'm not really like Englebert (Humperdinck). I don't just write ballads." And that kept me hanging on; but at the time, I tell you, it hurt me.'

As he said, Linda and his mates picked him up again, got him to believe in himself again and soon he was back on the road. Then, there was another stutter. The second Wings single was a version of the old nursery rhyme, 'Mary Had A Little Lamb', with updated music by McCartney. It was all very Paul, going family minded, but this piece of paternal indulgence was too much, even for his fans. It only rose as far as number five in the British charts. The abuse from the hard-nosed music press was universal.

Wings had yet to tour. This time the romance of McCartney came to the fore. The band were fully rehearsed but untried before an audience; so in February, 1972, Wings together with Paul with wife, three children and dogs set off in a large caravan for two weeks of concerts around Britain. Just like travelling players, they would stop in a university town, make themselves known to the local student body and ask if they could play. Naturally, no one was going to pass up such an opportunity.

Nottingham was the first venue, and Wings continued to eight more universities. It was a successful ice-breaker for the band, though they had to work hard in some places to get the audience to sit up. As a launch for the new face of Paul McCartney, it was not to be sniffed at. The romance of the great ex-Beatle playing free and without advance publicity was appealing, even though, by the end of the tour, the press were aware of their every move.

Paul McCartney and Wings were given an official launch in London before the band set off on a twenty-six date, seven-week tour of Europe. It was a tough schedule, but really brought the band together as a working unit. Paul had learned his Beatle lessons well. Tough as the tour was, it bore no relation to the gruelling, soul-destroying route marches of Beatlemania; there were enough rest-periods to keep sanity. Paul got busted for cannabis possession while in Gothenburg and had to pay £800, and the following year was fined £100 for growing the illegal weed on his Scottish farm. No one seemed to hold it against him.

The group's next single, 'Hi, Hi, Hi', was also banned by BBC radios 1 and 2. Perhaps with the publicity given to the European drug incident and the news that their cannabis had been sent daily by post from London, the BBC felt the song's title suggested inappropriate sentiments. It reached number five in Britain and number ten in the USA.

From there on in, Wings became more successful. McCartney's next single was almost a Beatle-type number. 'My Love' reached number nine in Britain but hit number one in the US. There have been few number ones since, but his records have almost invariably made the top ten on both sides of the Atlantic. Wings' history, despite musician changes, has been full of gold and platinum records.

McCartney has hit high spots — as with *Band On The Run*. There have also been troughs, with such songs as the James Bond theme for *Live And Let Die*. But even that showed McCartney in his role as professional churner-out of saleable musical commodities; he fulfilled his brief admirably. His record sales are legion and he will continue to make music until he dies. He will play live audiences until circumstances deny him. That's the way he is made; he can do little else.

He is a genuine Anglophile and, while his ninety-eight per cent tax bill leads him to record abroad, Britain, and Scotland in particular, has remained his home. He tends to parade his wife and three daughters less, perhaps because he has less to prove these days. But his family is still very important and he has no public regrets about introducing Linda into his band, despite the warnings given by such people as Mick Jagger, that letting a wife into his musical life could 'blow his career'. McCartney responded, 'Although I didn't wish to blow my career, I thought it was more important to get on with living.' Such are the words of an experienced man.

Paul doesn't seem to miss the hysterical adulation he once inspired. Nor does he miss the manic analysis of his lyrics or the role as youth culture spokesman. He was always too nice to be a real culture hero. Even when he was arrested in Japan for cannabis possession, nobody seemed prepared to make him a martyr as they would have done John. Paul is just not that kind of leader.

The role was forced on him because he worked with Lennon, and the two of them wrote songs which spoke clearly to a generation. Since the late Sixties, his solo songs have never quite made it to those former heights. But McCartney professes not to worry about that. In the words of his own composition, he now elects for 'Silly Love Songs'. 'What's wrong with that?' he asks in song. But you wonder why he needs to defend himself quite so vigorously. Why ask the question, unless he has the sneaking suspicion that really he *does* have more to offer. . . .

8 John: Yoko and Me—That's Reality

It was all over bar the shouting. But the shouting, or rather the barbed remarks were to carry on for some time. John had brought in Allen Klein to try and sort out The Beatles' business difficulties and to clean up Apple. Klein was a hard, aggressive businessman with no concern for the niceties of form or board room politeness. Lennon responded to that. He believed in him. He seemed to suspend judgement of the man and his methods and identified with him as the strong figure who would clear up the mess.

Lennon had, in fact, been the first to announce that he was leaving for good, but had held back on the announcement at Klein's request. He was, therefore, enraged at Paul's manoeuvre to get in his own announcement first. But, as the flurry of legalities continued, Lennon pursued the partnership with Yoko that had begun back in 1968. By mid-1970, when The Beatles split was announced, John and Yoko had already released four albums, mostly of electronic music, and three singles.

The singles, 'Give Peace A Chance', 'Cold Turkey' and 'Instant Karma', had been credited to The Plastic Ono Band. The name had been given jokingly to the perspex hi-fi cabinets in his Apple office; the group listed on 'Give Peace A Chance' did not exist. Eventually, real musicians took over the name when guesting for Lennon, as did Klaus Voormann and Eric Clapton, but it was simply a convenient handle.

John and Yoko put on art shows together. In March, an exhibition at the Robert Frazer Gallery of John's lithographs, showing his love-making positions with Yoko, was closed. The exhibits were seized by the police on grounds of obscenity.

The two continued to campaign for peace, remaining as love/hate figures for the press, for whom their antics supplied endless copy. They were treated with a kind of superior, moralising indulgence and sold to the public as a species of high-minded loony.

John's attacks on Paul, his role in the court case to wind up The Beatles and his music were quoted everywhere. The recriminations were sad but normal: it was a very public divorce. John was always, by nature, likely to be the most publicly brutal about the break-up. It was entirely consistent for the blunt Beatle to be as true to his feelings here as elsewhere.

Nor was it surprising that John and Yoko should continue regardless. With The Beatles out of the way, they were now free to pursue their activities full-time. John's career from then on was, in a sense, predictable, too. As a person, he was moody, complex, hard to motivate and erratically brilliant. His subsequent journeys reflected all that.

It is difficult, and possibly wrong, to extricate John's activities from his partnership with Yoko, since they saw themselves as two parts of one whole. But Lennon was a person in his own right and therefore had his own existence, albeit an existence very much bound up with that of his wife.

His post-Beatle life has three distinct phases. The first lasted until 1973, when the partnership operated on full steam; then, Yoko kicked John out, and Lennon went on an eighteen-month bender, returning home in 1975 to become a proud house-husband, father and recluse until emerging in 1980 with a new album.

In December, 1970, John's first proper solo album was released: *John Lennon/Plastic Ono Band*. A simple rock album with few overdubs, it was Lennon being painfully transparent about his feelings. He used the album as an attempt both to come to terms with and to exorcise his past. In the spring of that year, he and Yoko had experimented with primal therapy, a system developed by psychotherapist Dr. Arthur Janov, in which patients travel-back in their minds to their earliest memories of babyhood, and relive, in a 'primal scream', that first moment of frustration when thwarted in their wishes by outside forces—a means, so went the theory, to release the blockages of the past. John claimed that the therapy enabled him to be free and open with his feelings as never before. Yoko found it less important

106

and had arguments with Janov. They had taken the therapy as an outlet from their own relationship, which was becoming so obsessive and possessive as to be suffocating.

For Lennon, it was a temporary phase, but the *John Lennon/ Plastic Ono Band* album was a direct result of the therapy. He managed to write properly about his mother for the first time: 'Mother, you had me but I never had you', he sang, ending with a scream of anguish that released the tensions and disappointments of the past. But, although Lennon's adoption of Janov lasted not much longer than his discipleship to the Maharishi (Yoko said that, in both cases, John was looking for a daddy), the album said something about his and Yoko's beliefs which remained true to the end. In a song called 'God', Lennon chanted a kind of litany of past influences and, one by one, threw them away: 'I don't believe in Jesus . . . Bible . . . I Ching . . . kings . . . tarot . . . Zimmerman (Dylan) . . . Elvis . . . Beatles', to name just a few. At the end, a pause was followed by a sung statement of faith: 'I just believe in me, Yoko and me. And that's reality.'

That was Lennon's cardinal belief. In order to do anything, he maintained, you had to believe in yourself first. That was the basis of all further negotiations. At the close of the last interviews, given before his death in December, 1980, he reiterated the statement made on that first solo album: 'That's what I'm saying now, produce your own dream . . . You have to do it yourself. That's what the great masters and mistresses have been saying ever since time began. They can point the way, leave signposts and little instructions in various books . . . I can't wake you up. *You* can wake you up.'

Earlier on in the same song, 'God', he had sung, 'The dream is over'. He meant the dream of the Sixties, the notion that The Beatles, or any other rock group, could change the world, the myth that some new age could be ushered in by the counterculture. He commented at the time: 'The people who are in control and in power, and the class system and the whole bull-shit bourgeois scene is exactly the same . . . The dream is over. It's just the same, only I'm thirty and a lot of people have got long hair, that's all.'

But self-aware, often indulgently so, John and Yoko still felt compelled to preach peace to the world. They still had a desire to communicate. In order to do this better, Lennon shrugged off his old metaphors and images, and came straight to the point, with a transparent honesty that had never been in Paul's work. It is easy to chart Lennon's shifts in attitude and preoccupation through his music; Paul always concealed his.

After a while, that kind of open, confessional music becomes a bore. It was not so much that Lennon felt his audience were really interested in the details of his psyche, but that, having felt cramped by The Beatles for so long, he indulged in the opportunity to be *real,* to be himself.

It was revealing, but ultimately a turn-off, coming across as a therapy session for John. He did not use the music to sublimate his feelings, or use his feelings to make music that others could really identify with; there was too much John and not enough music. He was using his music as a vehicle, a propaganda weapon. The music suffered and the audience became bored with John's soul baring.

He made a second, more moderate album the next year: *Imagine.* As John said, 'It was working class hero (a song on the first album) with chocolate on.' In the earlier song, he had berated society for castrating the individual with 'religion, sex and TV'. In the title track of *Imagine,* he proposed the utopian alternative: 'Imagine there's no heaven, no religion, no countries, no possessions'. By his own admission, it was sugar-coated revolution. It was released in September, 1971, by which time he and Yoko had left their mansion in Ascot, Surrey and settled in Greenwich Village, New York.

Initially, they had come in a search of Kyoko, Yoko's daughter from her first marriage. Her former husband, Tony Cox, had disappeared with the girl, feeling very strongly that the environment and lifestyle of John and Yoko did not provide a healthy atmosphere for a child to grow up in. But Yoko missed her daughter and finding her became an obsession.

The custody battle that ensued lasted for years, with private detectives pursuing Cox and Kyoko in an effort to bring her back. In the end, it was settled by a ruling that Kyoko and Cox should stay together.

John and Yoko's arrival in New York marked the beginning of another shift in direction. John came in contact with two of the leading figures of the radical left, Jerry Rubin and Abbie Hoffman. Catching their enthusiasm for revolution, he went through a political transformation. Just as had happened with the Maharishi, he met them halfway. His own feelings about revolution had been reflected in his quandary over the song 'Revolution' — should he count himself in or out? This time, he reversed his decision. He counted himself in. But he was in a dilemma over violence. He felt uncomfortable about advocating violent political change but was unsure how radical change could be effected without it. 'You can't take power without a struggle,' he confessed.

In this mood, he and Yoko joined up with a band called Elephant's Memory, recording a double album, *Sometime In New York City,* released in April, 1972. It was an unashamed piece of propaganda, dealing with Angela Davis, the Attica prison revolt, Northern Ireland and Women's Liberation. But the writer who had once sung that people carrying pictures of Chairman Mao 'ain't going to make it with anyone, anyhow', now sporting a Mao badge, knew in his head that he was playing games. He knew that music should work on a deeper level. Radicalism, he said later, 'almost *ruined* it, in a way. It became journalism and not poetry.'

By this time, Lennon had another struggle on his hands. In February, 1972, his United States visa had run out. The Nixon administration, at its most paranoid, invoked John's October 1968 marijuana conviction as a reason to refuse the issue of a 'Green Card' immigration permit. There were rumours that Nixon had personally ordered government officials to harass Lennon and 'kick him out of America'. It is reported that they feared his presence as a radical leader and 'guerilla' in the field of culture. There began a legal wrangle that was not to be concluded until 1976. In the meantime, Lennon could not leave the country for fear that he would not be allowed back in. In 1973, the Federal Government ordered John's deportation, but Lennon's lawyer sued the government for wire-tapping and harassment and the press exploded with rumours of a conspiracy against Lennon.

Life carried on with benefit concerts and, in November, 1973, the release of an album, *Mind Games.* The songs had lost their radical edge and zeal, as he returned to introspection, John described it as 'an interim record, being between a manic political lunatic and back to being a musician again.'

By the winter of 1973, John and Yoko had separated. Circum-stances surrounding the split are confusing, but it apparently had a lot to do with their marriage roles. Despite his radicalisation and despite his co-operation in the feminist song, 'Woman Is The Nigger Of The World' (from *Sometime in New York City*), he was still expecting, in Northern, working men's fashion, to take the dominant role in the relationship. Yoko said that she had always been independent and strong-willed but couldn't cope with someone as strong, successful, famous and wealthy as John. She felt emasculated and her work suffered. Although it seemed at the time that Lennon had simply left, they both agreed later that Yoko had kicked him out.

Lennon says he wanted to return very soon after, and continued to 'phone Yoko, asking to be reunited. She told him: 'You're not ready to come home.' In pain and loneliness, Lennon hit the bottle, just as he had following his mother's death when he was at art school. He said, 'I tried to drown myself in the bottle.' Even then he was, in his own words, killing himself 'in a macho way'. Hanging out with a heavy drinking crowd, he was often in the papers for getting thrown out of this or that club and getting into fights.

In an attempt to distract himself, he started to make an album of old rock'n'roll standards with producer Phil Spector. But Spector turned funny toward the end of the sessions — retired to his house and locked up the tapes.

Lennon had spent most of his time hanging out with the music crowd in Los Angeles. Finally, he decided to return to New York and there he began to write again. Once more, he exorcised the pain of his immediate past, and put together an album called *Walls And Bridges*, released in October, 1974. The hit single taken from the album was a sad anthem to the previous year: 'Whatever Gets You Through The Night'.

By this time, he had won back the Spector tapes, which were largely unusable. He added new material, and *Rock'n'Roll Music* came out in 1975. It was John Lennon reliving the more pleasant memories of his past with the old rockers in the last recording he would make for five years.

January, 1975, saw the final, legal dissolution of The Beatles, and John back with Yoko in the fifty room apartment in the Dakota, in New York. They had met at Elton John's Thanksgiving Day Concert at Madison Square Garden and were reconciled. The relationship was now built on a new foundation — equality.

John said that he felt tied by contracts and the constant pressure (sometimes self-exerted) to record: 'Rock'n'roll wasn't fun any more.' He felt he'd become a craftsman, rather than an artist. Yoko, he said, helped him reach the decision to rest. She told him he didn't have to record; no one was forcing him to. So, Lennon rested and Yoko began to take care of the Lennon/Ono business empire. Their properties and possessions had grown large and unwieldy over the years and required some management, as did the still unresolved immigration problems, as well as royalty payments and record deals.

Yoko had suffered a series of miscarriages and had been advised by doctors that she should not think of having children. But the couple were determined. They contacted an acupuncturist who told them to lay off smoke, drugs and drink and they would be all right. Yoko became pregnant in spring, 1975 and, despite gynaecological hazards — caused by past abortions and surgery — with rest and full-time care by John, she came through.

On October 7, 1975, an appeals court overturned the order to deport John. Two days later, to cap the ecstasy, an 8lb 10oz boy was born to Yoko — on John's birthday. They called him Sean. 'I feel as high as the Empire State Building', said Lennon. On July 27, 1976, Lennon was awarded his Green Card. He was now a legal, permanent resident of the United States of America.

The period dating from John's return to Yoko was a quiet one, despite the birth of Sean (who, with no intended slight on Julian, he considered his first born) and the granting of his long-awaited Green Card. In media terms, he became a recluse. He made no public appearances, except in court (cases surrounding The Beatles and John's own music still reverberated) and he recorded nothing. Rock'n'roll friends like Elton John and, lately, Paul McCartney would drop in when in town. With Paul he was friendly, but polite; they would drink and reminisce. He did not hold court, as he had when first arriving in the Big Apple. But there were reasons for his seclusion.

He and Yoko had come to an arrangement over the baby. She had told him: 'I'm carrying the baby for nine months and that is enough, so you take care of it afterward.' John, still luxuriating in the security of being with Yoko again, was amenable.

For almost five years, he became a househusband. With the help of a nanny, he brought Sean up, cooked bread and worked around the house. Yoko spent her days in the office section of the sprawling apartment, making deals and running her artistic career. John did not adapt easily to the new role, but he coped. He experienced something of what his first wife, Cynthia, must have felt in bringing up their first son, Julian — now a teenager. Having dedicated himself to the family, his life began to take on some of the aspects of that of his old partner, Paul McCartney. But Lennon was still concerned to drive away his past. He said that, even after leaving The Beatles, it took him years to leave them in his *mind*. He told Sean nothing of The Beatles; he was his father, not a Beatle.

He lived as a New York househusband until the end of 1980. When asked what he did all that time, he replied: 'I've been baking bread and looking after the baby. Everyone else who has asked me that question over the last few years says, ''But what *else* have you been doing?'', to which I say, ''Are you kidding!'' Because bread and babies, as every housewife knows, is a full-time job. After I made the loaves, I felt like I had conquered something. But as I watched the bread being eaten, I thought, ''Well, Jesus, don't I get a gold record or knighted or nothing?''' Now, he was more than just an intellectual feminist.

Yoko continued to fill his life. He used, in jest, to call her 'mother', and perhaps he saw that quality in her, as well as those of a lover, wife and teacher. 'She taught me everything I know. From the day I met her, she demanded equal time, equal space and equal rights. I'm thankful to her for my education . . . She is the answer to everything. Being with her makes me whole.'

After five years' silence, in 1980 Lennon surfaced to record once more. On October 24, a single, '(Just Like) Starting Over', was released. In view of subsequent events, its title and sentiments have the ring of tragic irony. 'It's called ''Starting Over'' because that's exactly what I'm doing. It took me forty years to finally grow up.' He and Yoko recorded an album, *Double Fantasy*, so titled to show the Lennon/Ono secret when 'two people picture the same image at the same time'. In the rash of interviews that followed his re-emergence from obscurity, he said that the album was intended for people of his own generation, those who grew up with him — though he hoped the kids liked it, too. 'I'm saying, ''Here I am now, how are you? How's your relationship going? Did you get through it all? Wasn't the Seventies a drag? Well, here we are, let's make the Eighties great.'''

The album was introspective but optimistic. More than that, it was sentimental. Yoko Ono said that the message of *Double Fantasy* was 'family, relationships and children'. Had John and Yoko, after all these years, found themselves in the same camp as the McCartneys? It seemed unlikely; one of Lennon's great fears was of becoming ordinary. Back in 1975, he had said, 'I have this great fear of this *normal* thing. You know, the ones that passed their exams, the ones that went to their jobs, the ones who didn't become a rock'n'roller.'

He had set his sights on survival — so different from the Lennon of the Hamburg nights, of the acid days, even of the more recent drunken brawls. 'It's better to fade away like an old soldier than to burn out. I don't appreciate worship of dead Sid Vicious, or dead James Dean; I worship the people who survive, Gloria Swanson, Greta Garbo.'

But it was not to be. On December 8, 1980, John Lennon was shot dead by one of his fans, Mark Chapman, outside his New York apartment. The world felt a numbness. When Lennon died, it was as if an important part of our minds, our memories, died too. His was the death of a part of British social history, the death of a hero and spokesman. There were world-wide scenes of mourning.

It is tempting to believe that Lennon died at a time when he had finally found himself, that his years of search for peace and reality had been rewarded. But it is not true. Lennon was perpetually on his way from one place to another — not so much searching, but roaming, picking up what comfort he could on the way. He had found love and a measure of stability by the end. But Lennon was not content. He wanted more. He wanted the world to resolve its differences. He wanted, in essence, a new world where it would all work out. Sadly he never found it.

9 The Dream Is Over

Tragically, only now can we look back on the partnership of Lennon and McCartney with any degree of certainty. Until December, 1980, there was a theoretical chance that the partnership might revive. In real terms, it was never on. But maybe, *just* maybe, on one of the evenings when Paul and Linda dropped by John and Yoko's Dakota apartment, in the course of drinking and reminiscing, John and Paul might have wandered off to the studio and doodled a song together for old time's sake. The sad fact is, that can now never happen or even be dreamed about.

With John's death, the partnership reached its historical conclusion. Like all good stories, the tale of Lennon and McCartney had its beginning, its middle and a dreadful end. All that remains now is to try and adjust to a world without John Lennon. No longer will there be a flurry in the offices of the music press at the news of another Lennon album. For, ten years after The Beatles broke up, the rock world still pricked up its ears at the sound of a new John Lennon opus.

He was always the one to spring surprises. It was he who was most alive to the adjustments in world temperature and atmosphere level. He always had something to say. Paul's albums, except in his first solo years, never really caught the press's imagination in the same way. He kept his old fans and, with Wings, made millions more. They knew what they were getting with Paul McCartney. However hard he might be to reach as an offstage personality, in the public eye he remained as he had always been — a nice ordinary guy who was also a big, big star.

Lennon, on the surface, was contrary and prickly — always ready for a new idea. Strangely, underneath he seemed easier to understand, possibly because he opened his heart to the public to such a remarkable degree. For all those who could not take his changing fads and hobby horses, millions more responded to his transparent, and often moving, honesty.

Perhaps one clue to the interest always aroused by a new Lennon project was the fact that the audience who had lived through the life of The Beatles (not least, rock journalists) recognised and identified with the changes Lennon was going through. For others, John's changes had been so much a part of their own growing-up process that any activity in the Lennon/Ono camp provoked the question, 'What on earth is he going to do *this* time?'

This business of growing up with The Beatles is not to be overlooked. It contains the clues as to why they became popular in the first place and why Lennon and McCartney's songs have remained with us, achieving a status that will be maintained well into the next century.

All songwriters are part of their time, but Lennon and McCartney were unique in that their time coincided with a period of intense youth ferment — a new generation establishing itself in an era when social values and attitudes were under reassessment. When The Beatles hit big in 1963, they did so not only because of their music but because many teenagers, having rejected their parents' heroes, were looking for figures who expressed *their* view of the world.

Teenagers' identification with The Beatles, as described earlier, meant that they accepted their music into their daily lives. Lennon and McCartney's songs were the background to many an adolescent's formative experiences, and those formative years are vital to the making of an adult life. Adolescence and early adult-hood are very impressionable stages. They are full of so many important experiences — awakening sexuality, falling in love, insecurity, peer group pressures, rebellion, and the dawn of new ideas. Values which are implanted in childhood come under close scrutiny by teenagers; attitudes on which adult life are based begin to take shape here.

For kids growing up in the mid- and late Sixties, The Beatles were very significant. The experiences they went through became interwoven with The Beatles and with the songs of John and Paul. The Beatles were their heroes; kids felt immediately that The Beatles were on *their* side. So the identification they had with the personalities and the identification they had with their music became as one. As The Beatles themselves developed, reacting in their own way to the changing times, so the music changed, too. It became more sophisticated and the songs themselves began to reveal more about the composers and their attitude to the world. The fans were carried along in the flow.

It was not simple cause and effect. Life is more complicated than that. The Sixties were a vortex of change. Shifts in image and fashion were tied up with a sense of rebellion and a need for young people to assert themselves. They were also linked with changing attitudes towards sexual morality and the desire for greater freedom. It all stemmed from the fact that, in the eyes of many of the young, the older generation had blown it, living by outmoded moral codes and traditions.

The young helped generate the libertarian atmosphere which The Beatles breathed in. But they had the confidence to take advantage of it. They then gave the less forthright young something to aim for. So The Beatles were both the influenced and the influential.

With this organic give and take, and with the appetite of the media for new faces, it was inevitable that The Beatles should become more than simply popular entertainers. As the generation became more articulate, exploring their environs and their psyche, so too did The Beatles, passing back their experiences in vivid colour and imagery in that most insidious of mediums — music.

Music lives in the mind and the emotions. It encapsulates feelings and moods. Lennon and McCartney's music did that job for the Sixties children. More than any other, theirs is the music we most closely identify with the period. The fact that The Beatles' music has been associated, in millions of minds, with the formative experiences of youth has assured its longevity. Its perpetual rediscovery by successive generations has meant that it has been kept alive outside the collective memory of one ageing section of the population.

That rediscovery has more to do with the actual *quality* of the music than with any other social or cultural factor. The press and TV ballyhoo that constantly surrounded The Beatles, their role as mass-media entertainers and the fact that they became much greater than the sum of their parts or their music, casts doubts as to whether Lennon and McCartney were all they were cracked up to be. Were they just two amateur songwriters hyped as leading popular geniuses of the mid-twentieth century?

Their music belies that. It was their originality, their ability, at a time when the rest of the British pop scene was in slavery to America, to create something *genuinely* their own that forged their initial success. Everything else was based upon that. At their best, when John and Paul were really working together, their songs stood out clearly in a class above anything that anyone else (with the exception of Bob Dylan) was doing.

They shared with Picasso, and other major artists, the ability to soak up the stimuli thrown at them by their environment: contemporary music, words, images and experiences all became re-ordered and re-distributed to spill out into great music. But it was essentially a partnership. It only really worked with the two of them. When they wrote together, sparks flew. Each with their individual genius was able to counterpoint the other, excesses held in check — a creative clash of opposites. What they produced is evidence of a pairing of minds that transcended the mechanics of the making. Once recorded, and placed in the imaginations of the listeners, these songs took on a life of their own.

Once Lennon's and McCartney's songs entered the public arena, only the copyright remained theirs. From then on, they were public property. The young public who took possession of the songs chose to cherish them in a way that they had done with only a handful of others, such as with Bob Dylan. It was they, not Lennon and McCartney, who invested in the music a greater significance. It comes back once again to the role of The Beatles as spokesmen and prophets for a generation without leaders. They attributed to The Beatles the hopes, fears and experiences of their own lives. In some senses, they were right, but in another they read what they wanted to see in the songs rather than what was actually there.

American Beatle fans were worse, in this respect, than the British. But then The Beatles were seen differently on either side of the Atlantic. The issues on which dissident American youth stood were clearer. They had Vietnam and segregated schools to deal with, for instance. They are less steeped in tradition and have a greater respect for rhetoric. Being a republic means, probably, that public figures have more status and influence.

117

The Beatles, from early on, were treated as leading figures in the American social revolution; they were imputed with the status of youth spokesmen by audience and media alike. This meant, in turn, that their songs were heralded as nuggets of wisdom — messages from the high priests to the faithful.

In consequence, developing ideas and shifts of nuance in the Lennon and McCartney songs became a social barometer. When Lennon died, the mourning in the States was as if for a leader or chieftain.

In Britain, where distinctions are blurred and where rebels are not put on pedestals but absorbed into the soft mass of British society, The Beatles were seen more as eccentrics who could be tolerated as long as they didn't get into the street and frighten the horses. The Beatles were still seen by the young as heroes and leaders, but they were folk heroes in the Robin Hood mould rather than the leaders of a radical movement.

Whatever the response, it was such that Lennon and McCartney became more than songwriters. Compared to any songwriting partnership of the past — be it Gilbert and Sullivan, Rodgers and Hammerstein, or Goffin and King — The Beatles stand out as socially significant in a quite unique way. The songs of the others live on in warm-hearted memory, but not in the way Lennon's and McCartney's will.

When, to all intents and purposes, the partnership broke up in 1968, the songs began to lose direction and, as they developed as individual writers, they began to lose their role. This, as has been said, was more true of McCartney. But it also applied to Lennon.

John, by virtue of his own inclination to make statements and espouse radical causes, kept the focus on himself. He still drew the young and leaderless but, as he himself understood, the following who remained faithful were in a minority. His attitudes were so personalised that he lost the broad appeal he and Paul together had inspired. Nevertheless, whether individuals agreed or disagreed with all or part of what he was about, he still provoked interest and attention as a spokesman figure.

Both he and McCartney have claimed that the best of the solo material written subsequent to The Beatles break-up is as good as anything they wrote together. This is surely not the case. They have both written very good songs — they are very talented individuals — but separately they could never compete on the same level.

A lot has been said about their co-written and individual songs and some consideration given to their overall contribution to society. The Beatles did not have a highly developed sense of responsibility to their audience. They believed that everyone should be left to live his own life.

John's concern for global peace was worthy and his and Yoko's antics at least made it something of an issue, even if it became lost as the attention focused inevitably on the personalities rather than on the subject. Apple was a genuine, if misguided, attempt at taking the pressure of commercialism of the arts and both Lennon and McCartney gave considerable sums to organisations and groups concerned with the betterment of society. Almost all John's live performances, post-Beatles, were benefits and, in his last years, he and Yoko tithed their considerable earnings to charity.

Their music was itself a source of joy and beauty — an influence that can scarcely be quantified. But, on the other hand, their early public experiments with mind-bending drugs did little to help anyone anywhere. Their own experiments in promiscuity were self-evidently counter-productive and wasteful. Both Lennon's and McCartney's eventual realisation that a stable marriage and family relationships were crucial to individual serenity says a great deal about the sexual hedonism of the Sixties and Seventies.

But John Lennon and Paul McCartney just lived. It so happens that it all took place in the glare of global publicity. Such pressures do not make for a normal life and it is significant that both Paul, in his retreat to his Argyllshire homestead, and John, in his five-year seclusion in New York, *had* to duck out of the limelight for the sake of their own survival.

In assessing their lives and work, it is impossible to ignore the fact that, however much they influenced or were influenced, they had nothing special to offer by way of a solution to the world's problems. They were as lost as any of the generation they spoke for. In a frighteningly short period of time, they ran the gamut of possibilities: drink, drugs, sex, mysticism, politics, art, music and psychology, not really knowing what they were looking for or, indeed, if they were looking at all. In the end, they both opted for a kind of truce — a modicum of peace and security away from the mad world, centred around the family unit. Who would have thought, in the heady days of flower power, that this might be their ultimate option?

All Lennon and McCartney did, or claimed to do, was to make good records. That is certainly true. They were responsible for creating the best. They did not wish to start a new religion or a new party because that would mean providing the answers. They told the rest of us, 'It's up to you.'

In an interview, shortly before he was murdered, John looked back over his career and said, 'If The Beatles or the Sixties had a message, it was to learn to swim. Period. And once you learned to swim, swim.'

Every man for himself. I've heard that somewhere before.

Discography

THE BEATLES' SINGLES
(on Parlophone)

Love Me Do/P.S. I Love You
Oct 62

Please Please Me/Ask Me Why
Jan 63

From Me To You/Thank You Girl
April 63

She Loves You/I'll Get You
Aug 63

I Want To Hold Your Hand/This Boy Nov 63

Can't Buy Me Love/You Can't Do That March 64

A Hard Day's Night/The Things We Said Today July 64

I Feel Fine/She's A Woman
Nov 64

Ticket To Ride/Yes It Is April 65

Help!/I'm Down July 65

Day Tripper/We Can Work It Out Dec 65

Paperback Writer/Rain June 66

Yellow Submarine/Eleanor Rigby
Aug 66

Penny Lane/Strawberry Fields Forever Jan 67

All You Need Is Love/Baby, You're A Rich Man July 67

Hello, Goodbye/I Am The Walrus
Nov 67

Lady Madonna/That Inner Light
March 68

(on Apple)

Hey Jude/Revolution Sept 68

Get Back/Don't Let Me Down
April 69

The Ballad of John and Yoko/ Old Brown Shoe June 69

Come Together/Something
(Harrison) Oct 69

Let It Be/You Know My Name
March 70

THE BEATLES' ALBUMS
(on Parlophone)

Please Please Me: May 63
I Saw Her Standing There
Misery
Ask Me Why
Please Please Me
Love Me Do
P.S. I Love You
Do You Want To Know A Secret
There's A Place
Anna
Chains
Boys
Baby It's You
A Taste Of Honey
Twist And Shout

With The Beatles: December 63
It Won't Be Long
All I've Got To Do
All My Loving
Don't Bother Me

Little Child
Hold Me Tight
I Wanna Be Your Man
Not A Second Time
Till There Was You
Please Mister Postman
Roll Over Beethoven
You Really Got A Hold On Me
Devil In Her Heart
Money

A Hard Day's Night: July 64
A Hard Day's Night
I Should Have Known Better
If I Fell
I'm Happy Just To Dance With
    You
And I Love Her
Tell Me Why
Can't Buy Me Love
Any Time At All
I'll Cry Instead
Things We Said
When I Get Home
You Can't Do That
I'll Be Back

Beatles For Sale: December 64
No Reply
I'm A Loser
Baby's In Black
I'll Follow The Sun
Eight Days A Week
Every Little Thing
I Don't Want To Spoil The Party
What You're Doing
Rock And Roll Music
Honey Don't
Mr. Moonlight
Kansas City
Words Of Love
Everybody's Trying To Be My
    Baby

Help!: August 65
Help!
The Night Before
You've Got To Hide Your Love
    Away
I Need You (Harrison)

Another Girl
You're Going To Lose That Girl
Ticket To Ride
It's Only Love
You Like Me Too Much
Tell Me What You See
I've Just Seen A Face
Yesterday
Act Naturally
Dizzy Miss Lizzy

Rubber Soul: December 65
Drive My Car
Norwegian Wood
You Won't See Me
Nowhere Man
Think For Yourself
The Word
Michelle
What Goes On
Girl
I'm Looking Through You
In My Life
Wait
If I Needed Someone
Run For Your Life

Revolver: September 66
Taxman
Eleanor Rigby
I'm Only Sleeping
Love You To
Here, There And Everywhere
Yellow Submarine
She Said She Said
Good Day Sunshine
And Your Bird Can Sing
For No One
Dr. Robert
I Want To Tell You
Got To Get You Into My Life
Tomorrow Never Knows

**Sergeant Pepper's Lonely Hearts
    Club Band:** June 67
Sergeant Pepper's Lonely Hearts
    Club Band
With A Little Help From My
    Friends
Lucy In The Sky With Diamonds

122

Getting Better
Fixing A Hole
She's Leaving Home
Being For The Benefit Of Mr. Kite
Within You, Without You
When I'm Sixty-Four
Lovely Rita
Good Morning, Good Morning
A Day In The Life

THE BEATLES' ALBUMS
(on Apple)
The Beatles (Double Album):
   November 68
Back In The U.S.S.R.
Dear Prudence
Glass Onion
Ob-la-di, Ob-la-da
Wild Honey Pie
The Continuing Story of Bungalow
   Bill
While My Guitar Gently Weeps
Happiness Is A Warm Gun
Martha My Dear
I'm So Tired
Blackbird
Piggies
Rocky Raccoon
Don't Pass Me By
Why Don't We Do It In The
   Road
I Will
Julia
Birthday
Yer Blues
Mother Nature's Son
Everybody's Got Something To
   Hide Except Me And My
   Monkey
Sexy Sadie
Helter Skelter
Long Long Long
Revolution 1
Honey Pie
Savoy Truffle
Cry Baby Cry
Revolution 9
Good Night

Yellow Submarine: January 69
Yellow Submarine
Only A Northern Song
All Together Now
Hey Bulldog
It's All Too Much
All You Need Is Love
Pepperland
Sea Of Time
Sea Of Holes
Sea Of Monsters
March Of The Meanies
Pepperland Laid Waste
Yellow Submarine In Pepperland

Abbey Road: October 69
Come Together
Something (Harrison)
Maxwell's Silver Hammer
Oh! Darling
Octopus's Garden
I Want You (She's So Heavy)
Here Comes The Sun
Because
You Never Give Me Your Money
Sun King
Mean Mr. Mustard
Polythene Pam
She Came In Through The
   Bathroom
   Window
Golden Slumbers
Carry That Weight
The End

Let It Be: May 70
Two Of Us
I Dig A Pony
Across The Universe
I Me Mine
Dig It
Let It Be (version two)
Maggie Mae
I've Got A Feeling
One After 909
The Long And Winding Road
For You Blue (Harrison)
Get Back (version two)

COMPILATION ALBUMS

The Beatles/1962-1966 1973
The Beatles/1967-1970 1973
Rock'n'Roll Music 1976
Love Songs 1977
**The Beatles Live! At The Star
  Club In Hamburg, Germany:
  1962** 1977
**The Beatles At The Hollywood
  Bowl** 1977
The Beatles' Ballads 1980

EXTENDED PLAYERS

Magical Mystery Tour (two EPs)
  December 67
Magical Mystery Tour
Your Mother Should Know
I Am The Walrus
Fool On The Hill
Flying (Lennon, McCartney,
  Harrison, Starkey)
Blue Jay Way

PAUL McCARTNEY'S ALBUMS

McCartney: February 1970
The Lovely Linda
That Would Be Something
Valentine Day
Every Night
Hot As Sun
Glasses
Junk
Man We Was Lonely
Oo You
Momma Miss America
Teddy Boy
Singalong Junk
Maybe I'm Amazed
Kreen-Akrore

Ram: May 71
Too Many People
3 Legs
Ram On
Dear Boy
Uncle Albert/Admiral Halsey
Smile Away
Heart Of The Country
Monkberry Moon Delight
Eat At Home
Long Haired Lady
Ram On
The Back Seat Of My Car

Wings Wild Life: December 71
Mumbo
Bip Bop
Love Is Strange
Wild Life
Some People Never Know
I Am Your Singer
Tomorrow
Dear Friend

Red Rose Speedway: April 73
Big Barn Bed
My Love
Get On The Right Thing
One More Kiss
Little Lamb Dragonfly
Single Pigeon
When The Night
Loup (1st Indian On The Moon)
Hold Me Tight
Lazy Dynamite
Hands Of Love
Power Cut

Band On The Run: November 73
Band On The Run
Jet
Bluebird
Mrs. Vandebilt
Let Me Roll It
Mamunia
No Words (For My Love)
Picasso's Last Words (Drink To
  Me)
Nineteen Hundred And Eighty-Five

124

Venus And Mars: May 75
Venus And Mars
Rock Show
Love In Song
You Gave Me The Answer
Magneto And Titanium Man
Letting Go
Venus And Mars—Reprise
Spirits Of Ancient Egypt
Medicine Jar
Call Me Back Again
Listen To What The Man Said
Treat Her Gently—Lonely Old
    People
Crossroads Theme

I've Just Seen A Face
Blackbird
Yesterday
You Gave Me The Answer
Magneto And Titanium Man
Go Now
My Love
Listen To What The Man Said
Let 'Em In
Time To Hide
Silly Love Songs
Beware My Love
Letting Go
Band On The Run
Hi Hi Hi
Soily

Wings At The Speed Of Sound:
    March 76
Let 'Em In
The Note You Never Wrote
She's My Baby
Beware My Love
Wino Junko
Silly Love Songs
Cook Of The House
Time To Hide
Must Do Something About It
San Ferry Anne
Warm And Beautiful

London Town: March 76
London Town
Cafe On The Left Bank
I'm Carrying
Backwards Traveller
Cuff Link
Children Children
Girlfriend
I've Had Enough
With A Little Luck
Famous Groupies
Deliver Your Children
Name And Address
Don't Let It Bring You Down
Morse Moose And The Grey Goose

Wings Over America:
    December 76
Venus And Mars/Rock Show/Jet
Let Me Roll It
Spirits of Ancient Egypt
Medicine Jar
Maybe I'm Amazed
Call Me Back Again
Lady Madonna
The Long And Winding Road
Live And Let Die
Picasso's Last Words
Richard Cory
Bluebird

Wings' Greatest: December 78
Another Day
Silly Love Songs
Live And Let Die
Junior's Farm
With A Little Luck
Band On The Run
Uncle Albert/Admiral Halsey
Hi Hi Hi
Let 'Em In
My Love
Jet
Mull Of Kintyre

Back To The Egg
Reception
Getting Closer
We're Open Tonight
Spin It On
Again And Again And Again
Old Siam, Sir
Arrow Through Me
Rockestra Theme
To You
After The Ball/Million Miles
Winter Rose/Love Awake
The Broadcast
So Glad To See You Here
Baby's Request

McCartney II: May 80
Coming Up
Temporary Secretary
On The Way
Waterfalls
Nobody Knows
Front Parlour
Summer's Day Song
Frozen Jap
Bogey Music
Darkroom
One Of These Days

JOHN LENNON ALBUMS

Unfinished Music No. 1: Two Virgins November 68
Two Virgins
Two Virgins No. 1
Together
Two Virgins No. 2
Two Virgins No. 3
Two Virgins No. 4
Two Virgins No. 5
Two Virgins No. 6
Two Virgins
Hushabye Hushabye
Two Virgins No. 7
Two Virgins No. 8
Two Virgins No. 9
Two Virgins No. 10

Unfinished Music No. 2: Life With The Lions: May 69
Cambridge 1969
Song For John
Cambridge 1969
Let's Go On Flying
Snow Is Falling All The Time
Mummy's Only Looking For Her Hand In The Snow
No Bed For Beatle
Baby's Heartbeat
Two Minutes' Silence
Radio Play

Wedding Album: October 69
John And Yoko
Amsterdam

The Plastic Ono Band—Live Peace In Toronto 1969: December 69
Introduction Of The Band
Blue Suede Shoes
Money (That's What I Want)
Dizzy Miss Lizzie
Yer Blues
Cold Turkey
Give Peace A Chance
Don't Worry Kyoko (Mummy's Only Looking For Her Hand In The Snow)
John, John (Let's Hope For Peace)

John Lennon/Plastic Ono Band: December 70
Mother
Hold On (John)
I Found Out
Working Class Hero
Isolation
Remember
Love
Well Well Well
Look At Me
God
My Mummy's Dead

Yoko Ono/Plastic Ono Band
Why
Why Not
Greenfield Morning I Pushed An
   Empty Baby Carriage All Over
The City
AOS
Touch Me
Paper Shoes

Imagine: September 71
Imagine
Crippled Inside
Jealous Guy
It's So Hard
I Don't Want To Be A Soldier
   Mama, I Don't Want To Die
Give Me Some Truth
Oh My Love
How Do You Sleep?
How?
Oh Yoko!

Fly: September 71
Midsummer New York
Mind Train
Mind Holes
Don't Worry Kyoko
Mrs. Lennon
Hirake (previously Open Your Box)
Toilet Piece/Unknown
O' Wind (Body Is The Scar Of
   Your Mind)
Airmale (Tone Deaf Jam)
Don't Count The Waves
You
Fly
Telephone Piece

Sometime In New York City:
   June 72
Woman Is The Nigger Of The
   World
Sisters, O Sisters
Attica State
Born In A Prison
New York City
Sunday Bloody Sunday
The Luck Of The Irish

John Sinclair
Angela
We're All Water
Cold Turkey
Don't Worry Kyoko
Well (Baby Please Don't Go)
Jamrag
Scumbag

Approximately Infinite Universe:
   January 73
Yang Yang
Death Of Samantha
I Want My Love To Rest Tonight
What Did I Do?
Have You Seen A Horizon Lately
Approximately Infinite Universe
Peter The Dealer
Song For John
Catman (The Rosies Are Coming)
What A Bastard The World Is
Waiting For The Sunrise
I Felt Like Smashing My Face In A
   Clear Glass Window
Winter Song
Kite Song
What A Mess
Shirankatta (I Didn't Know)
Air Talk
I Have A Woman Inside My Soul
Move On Fast
Now Or Never
Is Winter Here To Stay?
Looking Over From My Hotel
   Window

Mind Games: November 73
Mind Games
Tight A$
Aisumasen (I'm Sorry)
One Day (At A Time)
Bring On The Lucie (Freda People)
Nutopian International Anthem
Intuition
Out The Blue
Only People
I Know (I Know)
You Are Here
Meat City

Walls and Bridges: September 74
Going Down On Love
Whatever Gets You Thru The
  Night
Old Dirt Road
What You Got
Bless You
Scared
No. 9 Dream
Surprise, Surprise (Sweet Bird Of
  Paradox)
Steel And Glass
Beef Jerky
Nobody Loves You (When You're
  Down And Out)
YaYa

Rock'n'Roll: February 75
Be-Bop-A-Lula
Stand By Me
Medley: Rip It Up
Medley: Ready Teddy
You Can't Catch Me
Ain't That A Shame
Do You Want To Dance
Sweet Little Sixteen
Slippin' And Slidin'
Peggy Sue
Medley: Bring It On Home To Me
Medley: Send Me Some Lovin'
Bony Moronie
YaYa
Just Because

Saved Fish: October 75
Give Peace A Chance
Cold Turkey
Instant Karma! (We All Shine On)
Power To The People
Mother
Woman Is The Nigger Of The
  World
Imagine
Whatever Gets You Thru The
  Night
Mind Games
No. 9 Dream
Medley: Happy Xmas (War Is
  Over)
Medley: Give Peace A Chance

Double Fantasy: November 80
(Just Like) Starting Over
Kiss Kiss Kiss
Cleanup Time
Give Me Something
I'm Losing You
I'm Moving On
Beautiful Boy (Darling Boy)
Watching The Wheels
I'm Your Angel
Woman
Beautiful Boys
Dear Yoko
Every Man Has A Woman Who
  Loves Him
Hard Times Are Over